Imagine That...

From PCs to NFTs

To Heidi —
Welcome to the future!
Thanks for all your help —
Beverly Macy
2023

BEVERLY MACY

Thank you -

To my family, friends, students, clients, employers, business partners, colleagues, and fellow travelers who have been part of my journey over the years.

And to all those blazing new trails into the NFT and Web3 universe and beyond - *you inspire me.*

ISBN: 979-8-88955-818-7

Table of Contents

Preface

Timing is everything, and *Imagine That... From PCs to NFTs* is a book for the current time that provides a comprehensive understanding of NFTs and their potential in the digital and virtual economy.

Through my experiences with emerging technology, I explore the evolution from personal computers to NFTs and the benefits creators, brands, and consumers could realize going forward.

The book also features nine transformative use cases from top brands and rising companies, which illustrate best practices in the NFT space. I am honored to include them here.

Glossary of Terms

The book starts with a Glossary of Terms, which is particularly important because NFTs and blockchain are relatively new concepts - many readers may not be familiar with the terminology used in this space. The glossary provides a concise and clear definition of the key terms used in the book, allowing readers to understand the concepts discussed and follow the narrative more easily. It also helps to avoid confusion and misinterpretation of the terms, ensuring that the reader fully grasps the ideas presented in the book.

Chapter 1: The Ownership Economy - *A New Renaissance*

This chapter delves right into the concept of the Ownership Economy and NFTs, going through how it has evolved and why it's becoming a significant force in the digital landscape. I discuss the migration from Web1 to Web2 and now Web3 and how creators, brands, and consumers can leverage these new developments to their benefit.

Chapter 2: The Arc from PCs to NFTs

This chapter explores the arc from personal computers to NFTs as it relates to my personal career. I was there at the advent of the personal computer through the dot-com era, onto social media, and now NFTs. I take a deep dive into how technology has evolved, leading to the emergence of NFTs and Web3 and their place in today's world.

Chapter 3: Strategies for Success

In Chapter 3, I outline strategies for success in the NFT and Web3 space. I examine different approaches creators, brands, enterprises, and consumers can take to leverage NFTs to achieve their goals and maximize their returns.

Chapter 4: Use Cases – Redefining Value

In Chapter 4, readers will hear about the exclusive and transformational Use Cases from top brands and rising companies. These cases range from media and entertainment to publishing, outer space, sports, financial services, and more. I highlight how NFTs are redefining value in these industries, changing the way we think about ownership and intellectual property.

Time Inc. – TIMEPieces - NFTs in Publishing

The ability of a 99+-year-old legacy brand like Time Inc. to not only re-invent itself via NFTs and Web3 but pave the way for others is absolutely brilliant. NFTs hit the radar of

Keith Grossman, President of TIME Magazine, in late 2020, and the rest is history.

Afrofuturism - NFTs and Art in Outer Space

One of the most iconic figures in the world of outer space and now of Web3 and NFTs, Dr. Sian Proctor, was launched into earth's orbit as the pilot of the Inspiration4 all-civilian mission to space on September 15, 2021. Being the pilot of this mission, Dr. Proctor became the first African American woman in history to pilot a spacecraft. Dr. Proctor has also played an important role in developing the genesis NFT collection as part of the Going to Space project.

Jenkins the Valet/Tally Labs - NFTs in Media and Entertainment

Jenkins the Valet is one of the first and most recognizable branded Bored Ape from the now-famous Bored Ape Yacht Club collection. The Jenkins the Valet project is a groundbreaking example of the potential of NFTs in the creative industry, as it is a written word project at its core. This potentially paves the way for other authors and writers to create and monetize their work using NFTs.

'All Time High' - NFTs in Music

Spottie WiFi, the creator of "All Time High', is a pioneering figure in the NFT music industry, and his work is helping to pave the way for the broader adoption of NFTs in the creative sector. Spottie is best known for his project that sold out in less than 60 seconds and netted him over $192,000, but he is also a guardian of the NFT space, dedicated to sharing his knowledge and experience with others.

Clube Atlético Mineiro - NFTs in Sports

Atlético Mineiro is the oldest active football club in Minas Gerais, Brazil, founded in 1908. This use case presents the benefits of NFTs: 1) as an investment, 2) as collectibles, 3) in ticketing, and 4) as a fan experience. Understanding that fans are passionate and hungry for as many of their favorite teams and their star athletes as possible is key.

VanEck Asset Management - NFTs in Financial Services

VanEck Assessment Management, an investment firm with over $82 billion in assets under management, entered the metaverse by releasing a collection of 1,000 NFTs in May 2022. The move represents a significant investment in the potential of NFTs by a major financial institution.

Three Squares Inc. - PledgeCrypto - NFTs in Environmental Services

PledgeCrypto, a platform that allows donors to make cryptocurrency donations to non-profits, commissioned an environmental impact assessment by Jaime Nack's firm Three Squares Inc. to quantify the carbon emissions of cryptocurrency transactions on its platform. They found that using the PoS model instead of the PoW model could reduce the carbon emissions of cryptocurrency transactions by up to 99.95%. These findings highlight the increasing demand for sustainable solutions in the cryptocurrency and NFT space.

Subtractive / St. Jude Children's Hospital - NFTs for Good

Combining NFTs and outer space is literally out of this world. The collaboration between Subtractive and Dr. Sian Proctor on the "Seeker" NFT project is a truly innovative and groundbreaking achievement that showcases the potential for combining NFT technology with outer space. The launch of the "Seeker" NFT on the Inspiration Flight not only marked a first in the world of NFTs but also helped raise money for a worthy cause - St. Jude Children's Hospital. In three days, they raised over $400,000, which exceeded all expectations.

Clutch Wallet – Crypto and Web3

Bec Jones, CEO and co-founder of Clutch Wallet, is working to provide education, insight, and information on Web3 for first-time users, with a particular focus on women. By offering a user-friendly and accessible way to learn about and engage with the Web3 ecosystem, Bec and the team at Clutch Wallet are helping to pave the way for wider adoption and understanding of this new technology.

Chapter 5 – Imagine That - Ready Player YOU

The chapter offers guidance on how to thrive in the virtual world through NFTs. I explore the growing virtual landscape and how individuals, companies, and brands can find inspiration in this new emerging world. It's a hopeful and exciting conclusion to the book's journey.

Understanding Intellectual Property in NFTs

This final chapter is authored by Intellectual Property attorney Natalia Aranovich and focuses on Intellectual Property and NFTs. This section provides essential legal insights and helps readers navigate the complex legal landscape of NFTs.

Introduction

I had to write this book. I was preparing for retirement from a career that has included software development, Corporate America, dot-com startups, entrepreneurship, emerging technology, co-writing a best-seller, and academia.

Everything was on track to wind down and spend more time with my family when I became aware of the NFT and Web3 space in March 2020. This new development symbolizes everything I am passionate about - emerging technology plus really smart and creative people redefining the status quo around ownership, money, and value at a very special moment in time. I couldn't resist. I had to write this book.

Imagine That... From PCs to NFTs is a follow-up to my first book, *The Power of Real-Time Social Media Marketing*, published by McGraw Hill in 2011. It is my vision of this New Renaissance and what it will mean to businesses, brands, and individuals.

This book is a sophisticated view of what is happening, why it is happening now, and what voices are rising up as leaders in this new worldwide journey. It will draw the readers' attention on how to identify and leverage significant trends in the development of NFTs and Web3 for their success and accomplishment.

This is more than a literary endeavor. The project will consist of the text of the book published in traditional formats, as well as a series of NFT experiences to include elements of art, music, and/or text that characterize the themes and reflect this unique moment in time.

The true power of NFTs and Web3 is taking shape before our eyes, and it is jaw-dropping. I recognize this as pivotal because I've witnessed similar moments before.

Spotting and leveraging trends early is something I've done throughout my career. In fact, I am often called upon to help decipher the emergence of new technologies and perspectives for the business world.

"You need this book. You will be smarter after reading it than you were before." That was the opening in the introduction of my last book, *The Power of Real-Time Social Media Marketing*, co-written with the amazing Teri Thompson. Social media was brand new, and it seemed that everyone was scratching their heads, wondering, "…how did this happen?" and "…what IS it anyway?". That book went on to be a bestseller. Over the years, it has been used in many universities and made the rounds with corporate executives and their teams.

Imagine That… From PCs to NFTs is even more important and also more significant. NFTs and Web3 are part of one of the most exciting and transformative developments in years. This unique and timely convergence of *culture, technology,* and *commerce* has changed how we look at intellectual property, ownership, provenance, royalties, digital and physical goods, money, and much more.

For those who are already involved in the NFT and Web3 world, the findings presented in this book will help broaden your understanding and open a window to additional opportunities on the horizon. For those who are new to the space, this volume will provide an introduction that should shed light on these bold new concepts. Whatever your position, you will feel the call to join in and learn more as the momentum builds for one of the most transformational times in recent history.

Imagine That... From PCs to NFTs is designed to educate, inform, and inspire the reader about the evolution of NFTs and Web3. It covers the current climate and also looks back on technological advances beginning with the advent of the personal computer in the 1980s. It covers the dot-com bubble, the beginning of social media, the introduction of NFTs and Web3, and what we might see next.

There is a massive shift underway – how we define ownership in the digital age, the way we work and live, where we work and live, and how we interact socially and professionally are all being redefined. We are more virtual and more digital than ever, as evidenced by the global adoption of digital tools from Zoom to telemedicine, to virtual concerts and conferences, to on-demand education and family gatherings. Add in NFTs, Web3, and the metaverse, and a new world perspective is emerging.

I have been fortunate to be at the forefront of major technology revolutions since the early 1980s. Throughout my professional life, I have observed each generation usher in massive disruptive innovations that have altered cultural sensibilities and prompted new ways of thinking.

It's one thing to track trends and gather information about an industry, competitors, new businesses, products, etc. It is another to turn that information into actionable intelligence that can have a strategic impact on the trajectory of a company. That takes a certain ability to be able to both function in the day-to-day and also zoom out 30,000 feet to see that larger landscape.

I began my career in software engineering for mini- and mainframe computers. In August 1981, IBM – the largest computer company on the planet at the time - announced the IBM 5150 Personal Computer[1], soon to become the IBM PC/XT, once the IBM 5160 was announced a bit later.

At that time, I was working for an IBM competitor, the infamous Wang Laboratories[2], which was a rising star in the field. The company had 33,000 employees and annual revenues of over $3 billion at its height. To this day, Wang Laboratories is remembered as a pioneer in the computer industry, and its innovations continue to have a lasting impact.

Dr. An Wang was a legend in those early days, and I had a chance to meet him at the Wang Labs headquarters in Lowell, Massachusetts. Dr. Wang was a modest man and a computer genius. In 1956 he sold his magnetic core memory patent (the predecessor to the silicon chip) to IBM for $500,000 and started Wang Laboratories.

Dr. Wang was the holder of many additional patents and, in 1984, was said to be worth $1.5 billion – a huge sum in those days. He and his wife were also major philanthropists, and he wrote a book entitled *Lessons* which was published in 1985.

Wang was way ahead of its time in many ways, with one of their commercials[3] even touting this "...*With our new electronic mail system, you can send all kinds of information from one part of the world to another...*" A direct predecessor to email! In 1985!

The company sold mini-computers and word processors, and I was on a team in the San Francisco Bay Area that provided solutions and support to U.S. Federal and U.S.

Military customers like NASA/Moffitt Field, Mare Island Naval Station, the Presidio Army Base, as well as U.S. Federal agencies, and so on.

In those days, a mainframe computer could literally take up an entire floor in an office building. They required a highly specialized and secure environment – not only to protect the data but also to protect the equipment itself.

Most of my colleagues and I didn't take anything other than mini- and mainframe computers seriously. We barely paid attention to the IBM announcement. Except I do remember wondering, "What are they thinking?" IBM didn't do much in those days without thinking it through and then thinking it through again.

This was the beginning of my life-long curiosity regarding trends and strategy. I remember thinking, "Why would IBM – who literally owns the worldwide computing market – take a risk like this? What are they seeing on the horizon that everyone else is missing?" That curiosity turned out to be one of the greatest assets I possess as it has allowed me to tune in to developing market currents with a strategic eye.

IBM always had all their ducks in a row and gamed out every move before making it. I began to wonder what they were up to with the IBM PC/XT. What did they know or see that others only scoffed at? Did they really think that scrappy startup Apple was a competitor? Or RadioShack, with the hobbyist's Altair computer? That just didn't seem to make good business sense. Did they really think people wanted a computer in their *homes*?

The general market response to the IBM PC/XT personal computer was… well… curious also. One of the brochures[4] for the product from 1981 touts, "My own IBM computer. *Imagine that.*"

But truth be told, most businesses had a substantial LACK of imagination at that time. In the early elite and arrogant days of Silicon Valley, big shots like Mr. Hewlett and Mr. Packard or the engineers at Intel were the bomb. They were smart, getting rich, and changing the way the business worked. Pretty heady stuff. No need to rock the boat.

For all that, some *did* have imagination, and the personal computer teams at IBM seemed to have a market perspective and vision that everyone else lacked.

Much is the same now. The current use cases for NFTs and Web3 are barely scratching the surface. I foresee that the continued evolution of NFTs will affect everything we thought we knew about ownership, business, money, assets, investments, value, utility, rarity, privacy, security, trust, creators, intellectual property rights, human interaction, artificial intelligence, space travel, and so much more.

As we stand on the doorstep of this massive shift in practically every area of our physical and digital reality, many are wondering what is considered a success today. How do legacy companies and brands navigate new working environments, greater transparency, virtual worlds, and more? How are digital identities being formed, and how will they interact in a virtual environment? What new business and career opportunities are opening up, and how best should companies, brands, and individuals prepare for them?

It is in times like these that we see communities form, ideas flourish, and businesses thrive. Of course, there is always risk in something new, and this nascent industry has already had its share of headline-making scams and risks.

However, don't linger on the sidelines too long. Stay curious and at least be open to new concepts and new ideas.

I promise this book will offer an inspirational view around these new, emerging technologies and offer fresh thinking on how brands and individuals can succeed in the digital age. It will help you make sense of what's happening and give you an edge on how best to position yourself, your organization, and your projects to achieve maximum results. *Imagine that.*

Glossary of Terms

Those new to NFTs and Web3 will feel like they need to learn a whole new language. They will want to refer to this Glossary of Terms over and over again to begin to understand both the language and what concepts it represents in terms of innovation.

For those somewhat familiar with NFTs and Web3, this Glossary of Terms will serve as a friendly reminder. This list is not exhaustive.

Key Concepts:

- NFTs are able to secure digital content, provide provenance, and embed conditional instructions via smart contracts – they reside on the blockchain
- NFTs are unique and one-of-a-kind, unlike traditional digital assets (such as a jpeg), which can be easily replicated and distributed
- Blockchain is a distributed ledger technology, and the underlying technology of Web3
- Cryptocurrency is the digital version of money, and creating 'tokens' is enabled by the blockchain
- IP (Intellectual Property) refers to "creations of the mind, such as inventions; literary and artistic works; designs; and symbols, names, and images used in commerce
- Creators 'mint' digital files into NFTs and post them on a marketplace for purchase
- Consumers (buyers) can buy, sell and/or trade the NFT

What is an NFT?

Think of an NFT as a digital collectible with a receipt of ownership and authenticity. An NFT is a digital receipt for any type of digital file - an artwork, an article, music, or even a meme. Eventually, anything and everything could be NFT'd - contracts, tickets, events, voting, health records, personal moments, and more.

Technically, an NFT is a non-fungible token that represents a certificate of ownership and authenticity for a digital asset (like art, video, or music) and permissions connected to that asset governed by a smart contract. The NFT resides on a blockchain and is immutable, which means it can't be changed.

What is a Blockchain?

A blockchain is a distributed, decentralized database that is shared among the nodes of a computer network. Blockchains are best known for their crucial role in cryptocurrency systems, such as Bitcoin, for maintaining a secure and decentralized record of transactions. The innovation with a blockchain is that it guarantees the fidelity and security of a record of data and generates trust without the need for a trusted third party. Ethereum became a popular blockchain for NFTs with its advent of the 'smart contract'. The market then expanded into other blockchains, such as Solana, Cardano, Polygon, and more are expected in the near future.

What is a Genesis Drop?

A Genesis NFT collection is the first set of NFTs released by a creator. It is also referred to as the Gen-1 release or the OG drop. These drops are usually associated with a number of perks, commonly known as utility in the crypto and NFT space.

What is Intellectual Property (IP)?

Intellectual Property refers to "creations of the mind, such as inventions; literary and artistic works; designs; and symbols, names, and images used in commerce." It also covers "NIL" name, image, and likeness. That means that in addition to your very own NIL, anything you make up or create – a song or melody, art, design, a book, a photograph – the list is endless – belongs to you by law.

What is Cryptocurrency?

A cryptocurrency is a digital currency, which is an alternative form of payment created using encryption algorithms. Bitcoin is the most famous cryptocurrency, and there are hundreds of others. The use of encryption technologies means that cryptocurrencies function both as a currency and as a virtual accounting system. A cryptocurrency wallet is required to store cryptocurrency tokens.

What are Smart Contracts?

Smart Contracts are programs stored on a blockchain (Ethereum) that run when predetermined conditions are met.

They are typically used to automate the execution of an agreement so that all participants can be immediately certain of the outcome without any intermediary's involvement or time loss.

What are NFT Royalties?

Royalties from NFTs give the original creator a percentage of the sale price each time the NFT creation is sold on a marketplace. In business, royalties generally pay the creator a percentage of sales or profits. With NFTs, royalties are usually set by the owner during the minting process and can be governed by a Smart Contract.

What is the Metaverse?

The metaverse is a core feature of Web3. The metaverse will be accessible through phones, computers, wearable tech, and headsets (or a combination of these), and it will be where you work and meet professionally, where you shop, exercise, socialize, and where you watch movies and concerts, game, travel, and more. Decentraland and Sandbox are examples of metaverse spaces. With millions of daily users, both Roblox and Minecraft also consider themselves part of the metaverse.

What is Web3?

Web3 is the current evolution of the Internet and represents the Ownership Economy. The term "Web3" refers to the entire ecosystem of decentralized computing, crypto, blockchains, NFTs, and metaverse(s). Web1 was the Information Economy – read-only, hypertext, AOL/Yahoo!.

Web2 is the Platform Economy - interactive, social, apps, Instagram/TikTok/AppStore.

What is Fungible/Non-fungible?

Fungible denotes goods like commodities, common shares, options, and dollar bills. Assets like diamonds, land, or baseball cards are not fungible because each unit has unique qualities that add or subtract value.

Non-fungible is a unique digital identifier that cannot be copied, substituted, or subdivided, that is recorded in a blockchain, and used to certify authenticity and ownership (as of a specific digital asset and specific rights relating to it.

What is a Crypto Wallet?

Crypto wallets store the owner's private keys, keeping cryptocurrency safe and accessible. The wallet also allows the owner to send, receive, and spend cryptocurrencies like Bitcoin and ETH.

What does 'Mint a Token' Mean?

In cryptocurrency, minting is a decentralized method that enables an individual to generate a new token without the involvement of a central authority, such as the government or the bank. It can either be a non-fungible token or a crypto coin.

What Does 'Tokenize an Asset' Mean?

The tokenization of assets is the process of issuing security tokens (a type of blockchain token) representing real digital tradable assets.

What is an Allow List?

An NFT Allow List (otherwise known as a whitelist) is a list of crypto wallet addresses collected via a Web3-enabled form that allows specific community members a guaranteed spot for minting a new NFT collection.

What is an Airdrop?

An NFT airdrop is a distribution of NFTs that are sent to a crypto wallet address for free. Airdrops can be used for promotion or to draw attention to a brand or experience.

What is a POAP?

A POAP (Proof of Attendance Protocol) is a unique NFT given to people to commemorate and prove they attended an event, either virtual or in real life (IRL).

What are 'Gas Fees'?

A gas fee is a charge that users pay to transact on the Ethereum blockchain. Gas is used to compensate miners for the computing energy and resources expended to validate transactions and to include them in the blockchain.

What is the Difference Between Decentralized vs. Centralized?

In a centralized network, all users are connected to a central server that stores complete network data and user information. In a decentralized network, there are several peer-to-peer user groups, each with its own separate server that stores data and information relevant to that particular group.

What are NFT Marketplaces?

An NFT marketplace is a digital platform for buying and selling NFTs. These platforms allow people to store and display their NFTs plus sell them to others for cryptocurrency or money. Some NFT marketplaces also allow users to mint their NFTs on the platform itself. Top marketplaces as of June 2022:

- OpenSea
- Rarible
- NBA Top Shot
- Nifty Gateway
- SuperRare

What is a Secondary Market?

The Primary market is where the creator lists the original NFT for sale. The Secondary market is where a collector, who has bought an NFT, can resell or relist their NFT. The content creator, or original artist of the NFT, earns royalties through subsequent sales in the secondary market.

What gives an NFT Value?

Among the factors that make NFTs valuable are their rarity, scarcity, utility, ownership history, underlying value, perception of the buyer, liquidity premium, and future value.

What is NFT Rarity?

NFT rarity determines how rare and valuable an NFT is. Collectors highly prize truly rare NFTs, which makes them more expensive. Consequently, people want to know whether the NFT they own is rare or whether the one they plan to purchase is rare.

What is NFT Scarcity?

Scarcity refers to how much of a particular project is available at any given time. It is about the supply. If supply doesn't meet the demand, it can cause a rise in price.

What is a PFP?

PFP or 'Picture for Proof' refers to the popular use of NFTs as literal profile pictures on social media sites like Twitter. It is often thought of as the owner's Avatar or Virtual Identity.

What are Discord and Twitter Spaces?

Discord is a chat site, and Twitter Spaces is a social audio feature of Twitter. Both are used for information sharing and community building in the NFT space.

What is NFT Utility?

NFT utility is the value or offering that's attached to an NFT. NFT utility includes things like digital assets, physical goods, a service, access to events, memberships, and any other perks the creator wants to supply to their consumers.

What is a DAO?

A DAO, or "Decentralized Autonomous Organization", is a community-led entity with no central authority. It is fully autonomous and transparent: smart contracts lay the foundational rules, execute the agreed-upon decisions, and at any point, proposals, voting, and even the very code itself can be publicly audited.

What is a Rug Pull?

A rug pull is a crypto/NFT scam that occurs when a team pumps their project's token before disappearing with the funds, leaving their investors with a valueless asset. Risk management is critical in this new space. Scammers are much more sophisticated these days, and the eye-popping sums making headlines attract all kinds of attention. In addition, cryptocurrency exchanges are under pressure to provide more safety in terms of guardrails and governance.

How to Mint an NFT With Current Technology

This is why it is so important to learn and understand everything you can about Web3 and NFTs. Let's review the process:

- The creator produces a digital asset file (music, art, photography, etc.)
- That digital asset is minted (uploaded) as an NFT token on a blockchain via an NFT marketplace (like OpenSea). That NFT is now immutable, which means it is time-stamped and can't be changed
- The NFT represents a certificate of ownership and authenticity for that digital asset and any permissions connected to that asset that is governed by a smart contract. Because the asset's activity is entered on the blockchain, the provenance is always secure. The "smart contract" further confirms this.
- When the minted NFT is purchased on the marketplace via a crypto wallet, the new owner could also be granted the digital rights to resell, distribute or license their newly acquired asset in any way they choose, depending on the elements in the smart contract.
- That NFT can be held by the owner (in a collection), or it can be sold or traded.

Chapter 1

The Ownership Economy - *A New Renaissance*

Imagine that everything in the real world and in the digital world – land titles, real estate, art, music, film, books, investments, passports, tickets to sports or music events, receipts - everything – could have a 'receipt' that represents proof of ownership, manages licensing of intellectual property (IP), provides social status, grants exclusive access, and certifies authenticity.

Not only is this possible, but it is also happening right now. We are witnessing a new renaissance with the advent of NFTs and Web3 in our business and personal lives.

The convergence of *culture, technology, and commerce* is sparking our worldwide imagination, and this significant development has the potential to greatly impact the way we use, trade, and exchange digital and physical assets. It is important for businesses and individuals to understand and adapt to this technology in order to take advantage of its many benefits.

NFTs are digital collectibles that come with a digital receipt proving ownership and authenticity. Think of it this way - customers store books from Amazon and songs from Spotify on their devices, but they don't actually *own* that book or song. They pay through a subscription service.

However, NFTs are owned by the consumer. With an NFT, it's like buying a limited edition collectible. The customer owns the unique digital asset (the specific book or song) and can enjoy it, display it, or resell it, just like a physical collectible. NFTs give assets a whole new level of ownership and value

In essence, NFTs are the 'digital receipts' that can be used to verify ownership and authenticity of a wide range of digital assets, including books, digital art, photographs, collectibles, music, film, investments, and even physical assets like real estate and luxury goods.

NFTs are stored on a "blockchain", a computer platform that helps keep track of who owns what. NFTs are special because they are one-of-a-kind and can't be replaced. The value of an NFT is determined by the creator and can be influenced by factors such as perceived rarity, digital scarcity, and market demand.

While an NFT of a book or music may not provide the same functionality as a traditional physical book or music, it does represent ownership and can be considered a form of investment.

Another example comes from the realm of real estate, where NFTs could be used to create a more secure and transparent system for managing land titles and property transactions. In the world of art and collectibles, NFTs could provide a new level of authenticity and provenance for digital and physical assets, increasing their value and making them more desirable to collectors.

Additionally, NFTs can be used to manage the licensing of intellectual property, giving creators more control over their work and ensuring they receive fair compensation for their creations. This is especially beneficial in the digital world, where it can be difficult to enforce copyright laws and protect creators' rights.

Consider the following:

- Nyla Hayes, a 12-year-old digital artist, was named TIMEPieces' first Artist-in-Residence after the iconic TIME Magazine launched TIMEPieces, a new NFT community initiative that includes art pieces from a wide-ranging group of over 40 artists from all over the world. The collection netted over $40 million+ in total sales volume. Nyla's compensation was truly life-changing for her and her family.
- Spottie WiFi, a musician and rapper, released an NFT project that generated $192,000 in 60 seconds - more money than he'd ever made from a full year of releasing music online.
- An NFT auction for charity was run from outer space by Dr. Sian Proctor, a geoscientist, explorer, space artist, poet, and astronaut who became the first black female pilot of an orbital spacecraft. Over $400,000 was raised in 24 hours.

The current NFT cycle has been a catalyst for a new renaissance, as it has enabled individuals who previously excluded from the traditional art market to participate and create new forms of digital art and collectibles. This has resulted in an explosion of creativity, innovation, and new forms of expression and will lead to further developments in the future.

It is speculated[5] that over 50 million people worldwide consider themselves 'creators' and participate in some way in what is referred to as the Creator Economy. The prolonged pandemic gave this Creator Economy an additional boost... right into the arms of the Ownership Economy. The digital assets they create – art, music, photography, books, etc., are registered (or minted) on Web3 Internet via blockchain technology and then monetized. The NFT is then the 'digital receipt' that tracks those assets as they are bought and sold.

The current Web2 social media platforms like Facebook, Instagram, and Snapchat enable these creators to produce content, build a fan base, and then monetize that fan base relatively easily – sometimes in massive numbers. But the platforms also take a cut and retain ownership of all the intellectual property.

Now through NFTs and Web3, value and ownership are assigned to the creator of the content and to their intellectual property. Think of that. As a creator, your content is valuable, and you own it. This potential for creators to retain ownership and control over their work, and to monetize their content through NFTs, is a major shift from the current model on Web2 social media platforms.

People all around the world are flocking together and connecting with one another via Discord, Twitter Spaces, and other community platforms discussing these new ideas, launching and supporting NFT projects, and sharing knowledge and experience. The energy is palpable.

In nature, a flock of birds is held together by an unseen glue that tells them when to dip and fly. Birds flock together for social interaction and companionship and to communicate with each other, and to build social bonds. A while back, it was discovered[6] that birds in flocks anticipate sudden changes in the flock's direction of motion. Once that direction begins, it spreads throughout the flock in a wave.

Sound familiar? That is how imagination and inspiration are fueling NFTs and Web3 - in waves that cannot be physically contained. This is incomprehensible and counterintuitive to most business professionals and legacy brands.

Many are wondering if this is just a fad. Is this truly a renaissance or something that will soon fade away? The rise of NFTs and Web3 technology has sparked widespread interest and excitement, with many people and businesses eager to learn more about this emerging technology and its potential impact on various industries. As more and more people become aware of the potential of NFTs to revolutionize the way we think about ownership and value, the enthusiasm and support of the community become crucial to the success of NFT projects.

Is this risk-free? No new technology or disruptive business process is risk-free. In fact, the NFT market has already seen instances of fraud, hacks, and other types of nefarious activity. Even so, NFTs have the potential to revolutionize the way we think about ownership and value in the digital world, and innovation marches on. Guardrails and policies to protect consumers will surely follow.

Culture, Technology, and Commerce

The rise of NFTs and the combination of value and ownership has launched a new era - that of *culture, technology, and commerce*. Each element alone has seen remarkable changes lately. These three elements combined are the dynamic force driving the New Renaissance and the

Ownership Economy and are providing new opportunities for creators to thrive in the digital world.

In 2020 and 2021, newly energized creators burst on the scene with their digital creations minted as NFTs on the blockchain. The combination of digital content and digital currency on the blockchain sent some creators into the stratosphere financially. For others, it opened up a wholly new process that provided a platform and opportunity to be heard, claim ownership, and monetize one's creations. It is slowly dawning on people that perhaps the concept of 'the starving artist' will finally begin to disappear from our vocabulary.

Culture: Culture refers to the growing community of artists, musicians, entertainers, gaming enthusiasts, brands, and others who are using the Internet to share their work and connect with audiences. With the advent of blockchain technology and NFTs, culture has expanded even further, giving creators new ways to establish the value of their work and monetize their creations.

For years, digital creators have been supremely frustrated by the fact that their content generates engagement and excitement on platforms like Instagram, TikTok, or Twitter, but they get very little in return. Or there's always a middleman involved – a record label, a publisher, a gallery ecosystem – and the revenue never seems to flow fairly.

NFTs now allow artists and other creators to establish the value of their work and then monetize that content. For the first time ever, they can protect their ownership online and may even receive royalties on the secondary market.

New marketplaces for art and digital assets have quickly emerged. Suddenly, we see headlines about celebrities like Reese Witherspoon or Snoop Dogg launching an NFT collection or the NBA (National Basketball Association) launching Top Shot, its own NFT marketplace. The race is on, and in many cases, the results have been breathtaking.

Technology: The crucial role *technology* plays in the evolution of the Internet is a critical component of Web3. The basis for Web3 is the blockchain, which was introduced in 2008. It was best known as the infrastructure supporting the cryptocurrency Bitcoin.

Blockchain technology and digital currency are the most significant technologies affecting the rise of NFTs. Together they enable ownership and immutability of digital content and assets. Their implementation in commerce can help businesses and creators find new revenue streams, improve transparency, and boost community engagement.

In 2015, the Ethereum blockchain came onto the scene, adding the concept of 'smart contracts' to the mix. Smart contracts are a special code connected to an NFT that indicates permissions and confirms the asset as unique, traceable, and verifiable. These smart contracts have opened up new opportunities for creators to protect their ownership and receive royalties on their work.

Commerce: In this context, commerce includes both the exchange of goods and services as well as the digital currency that currently drives the space. The adoption of digital currencies and the rise of NFTs has led to the creation of new marketplaces for art and digital assets where creators can sell their work directly to audiences.

The way we buy and sell goods and services has continued to evolve. It may be hard to believe, but just 20 years ago, e-commerce was still brand new. Consumers were highly resistant to putting their credit card information online. They also asked, "How can I buy shoes, tools, or clothes if I can't see them, touch them, or try them on?" Of course, those barriers were removed, and today we couldn't imagine life without e-commerce.

Fast forward to today, and we see that the adoption of digital currencies and Web3 Internet technology has accelerated commerce into a new era. The concept of buying and selling NFTs that are bought with digital currencies 'on-chain' is beginning to catch on.

Together, this convergence of culture, technology, and commerce is driving the development of Web3 and is helping to shape the future of the Internet. It is providing new opportunities for creators to thrive in the digital world and is helping to pave the way for the next generation of online communities and marketplaces.

Companies are beginning to use NFTs to encourage loyalty, reward customers for purchases, or provide access to exclusive events. Some use NFTs as a way to issue equity or raise capital for new ventures. Others are using NFTs for marketing campaigns.

By combining NFTs and commerce, creators and brands have the opportunity to produce high-level profit value and enhanced customer experiences. NFTs can also eliminate counterfeiting and fraud in the supply chain, and Web3 technology offers product authenticity verification, which can make it more profitable for the brand and safer for consumers.

The present adoption curve of NFTs and Web3 is similar to the growth of social media in the mid-2000s. At first, companies were suspicious of social platforms as a channel for customer engagement. One CEO commented, "Do you mean I have to pay someone to *TWEET* all day? That's not going to happen." These platforms were considered an interruption of 'real work', and it took years before companies accepted social media as part of their overall marketing and communications strategy.

The Historical Renaissance and the New Renaissance

There are compelling parallels to the historical Renaissance at play here as well. Today, in this New Renaissance, we see creativity and financial opportunity flourishing in art, photography, film, music, and more being generated as NFTs. We also see new currencies and new forms of commerce.

The historical Renaissance was a period of great cultural, artistic, and intellectual flourishing in Europe during the 14th to 17th centuries as well. It was a time of great change and innovation, and it saw the emergence of many of the cultural, artistic, and intellectual developments that we continue to value today. Some of the key characteristics of the Renaissance include the emergence of new artistic styles and forms and the growth of scientific inquiry and discovery.

During the historical Renaissance, the convergence of culture in the form of art and new approaches to commerce and finance were also abundant. Florence, Italy, in particular, prospered as a commercial center and was among the first cities to adopt a sophisticated banking system.

There was even the introduction of a 'coin' (token!) - the golden florin coin - which replaced the much less valuable silver coins of the time. The florin spread throughout Europe, and Florentines were even hired to oversee mints and mines in other financial centers. 'Mints' and 'mines' should also be terms that are recognizable today.

Because of the financial backing artists received, some ventured into new techniques and new 'technologies' of the day. Artists began to experiment with oil-based paints and the fresco technique – revolutionary for the time. Perspective and light were introduced – perfecting the sense of three-dimensional reality. The dramatic impact of using these techniques has changed the way we look at the world for all time. This could also easily describe the digital/virtual dimensions being created today.

Much is the same in our times. The New Renaissance and the creativity of the NFT artists themselves are incredibly inspiring. Take generative art, which is developed through creative coding. Essentially, the work's elements are created by the artist, and a unique computer code allows them to be generated with completely unique traits. Generative art projects often programmatically enforce a supply cap on the total amount of pieces that can be produced, which seems to be typically up to 10,000+ unique NFTs per collection.

The work that is just beginning to emerge is often stunning. Artists like David Bianchi are using new digital tools to experiment with creating layered art, music, and poetry that is truly brilliant. The inspiration driving artists is one of the most exciting parts of this new landscape. Today's market will be changed forever as digital assets, ownership, and creators continue to evolve.

NFTs appeal to brands, merchants, collectors, customers, and creators, particularly in industries such as toys, music, gaming, art, and sports. For example, NFTs are revolutionizing the art world. Using an NFT marketplace, artists can sell digital art directly to buyers, removing and/or reducing the role of a gallery or auction house. Artists are better compensated for their art on the original sale by eliminating the need for intermediators, who typically take a large percentage of the sale profits. Some smart contracts can enable artists to earn royalties each time their artwork or music is sold on secondary markets.

For those new to the space, some NFT concepts may seem hard to grasp at first. When the iPhone was introduced in 2007, very few understood the concept of 'Apps'. Apple made it easy by letting everyone know that 'Apps' would simply make their lives more convenient.

Fifteen years later, the smartphone of today pulls up banking and grocery apps, safety apps for parents of school children, or links to home security cameras. Not to mention the convenience of quick and accurate GPS navigation, immediate entertainment content, car lock/unlock features, fitness tracking, and health information. "There's an App for that" has become a constant refrain.

In a relatively short period of time, there is now more computing power in the smartphone in the palm of your hand than sent a man to the moon in 1969. Acceptance and adoption of new concepts forges its own path.

New NFT and Web3 developments are emerging every day. We will look back and realize how impactful this moment in time truly is for both creativity and new ownership business models.

As mentioned earlier, Web3 is the next phase in the Internet's evolution and encompasses all of these components. Here's a bit of history on that evolutionary process.

Web1 – The Information Economy

Web1 refers to the first generation of the World Wide Web, which was characterized by static, text-based websites and the lack of interactivity and user-generated content. Web1 emerged in the late 1990s and was dominated by large, established companies and organizations that used the web as a platform for sharing information and promoting their products and services.

Web1 was dominated by searches, domains, and websites, basically transferring what we did on paper onto the World Wide Web. It was read-only things like e-zines and blogs. Think 'surfing the web'. Some will even remember when America Online (AOL) CDs were actually mailed to every home in America. And who could forget the sound of a modem screeching as it tried to find a World Wide Web connection? That really sums up the Web1 experience.

Next came the emergence of Web Portals like Yahoo! and AOL, search engines like Google, and e-commerce sites like Amazon. Early search engines like Yahoo!, Ask Jeeves, Magellan, Lycos, Infoseek, and Excite dominated. Google adopted the idea of selling search terms in 1998 from a small search engine company named GoTo.com. That one idea changed Internet monetization forever.

The dot-com craze and crash between 1998 and 2000 epitomized the times. One of the important takeaways from Web1 was that consumers began to expect information delivered to them quickly and 'for free'.

Web1 was a crucial step in the development of the modern Internet, and it paved the way for the more dynamic and interactive Web2 that came after. Today, many of the websites and technologies that were popular during the Web1 era have been replaced by newer, more advanced versions, but the legacy of Web1 can still be seen in the way the web is structured and used today.

Web2 – The Platform Economy

Web2 refers to the second generation of the World Wide Web, which emerged in the late 1990s and early 2000s. It has been characterized by the increased use of web-based technologies and the emergence of social media, user-generated content, and interactive web applications.

Web2 is dominated by websites that highlight user-generated content, usability, and interoperability for end users. Think read-write. Web2 is also called the participative social web. It does not refer to a modification to any technical specification but more a modification to the way websites are designed and used. Interaction and collaboration with each other are at the core of Web2, creating a social media dialogue as creators of user-generated content in a virtual community. Twitter, Facebook, Instagram, Snapchat, TikTok, and other social media platforms typify Web2.

We've been in Web2 pretty much since the financial crisis of 2008/2009. Our lives today are digital and mobile, and we live on our screens and devices. We use these platforms 'for free'. All we had to do in the beginning was sign up with our personal data. That seemed fair at the time. Facebook offered access to potentially billions of users (customers) for free. Little did most users know that 'for free' was going to get very expensive later on in terms of a lack of privacy and security.

Web2 is centralized and controlled by BigTech and BigPlatforms. Centralized sites are wholly controlled by the platform owners. The technology is consolidated to better manage security, data management, and administration of data. Yes, Web2 platforms are free to use, but users sacrifice their privacy and data for convenience. Now that they control all your data, these centralized tech companies have been harvesting and manipulating the data to their advantage by selling it to advertisers, etc. It turns out that YOU are the product.

All this was made so much easier with the rise of the smartphone. Your smartphone now replaces cassette tapes, telephones, CDs, the Rolodex, branding and design, encyclopedias, classified ads in newspapers, newspapers, disposable cameras, yard sales, paper maps, health monitors, personal banking, investments, and so much more. Most of modern life could not continue without the smartphone.

The combination of your smartphone and BigTech's never-ending thirst for data to sell to their BigAdvertisers has become a nightmare for many. Consumers are now questioning the wisdom of their earlier decision and coming up with a big "NO WAY". "My data belongs to me" is the new mantra.

The rise of Web2 has had a significant impact on the way the Internet is used and has transformed the way people communicate, share information, and collaborate online. It has also created new opportunities for businesses and organizations to reach and engage with their customers and audiences in more meaningful ways.

Web3 - The Ownership Economy

Critical to Web3 is the concept of ownership. Your data and your IP belong to you. "Own your own IP" is the new mantra.

Is Web3 a PLACE or a THING? Well, "Is the Internet a place or a thing"? Web3 is the next evolution of the Internet – a virtual, digital environment enabled by blockchain technology that users can choose to participate in or not.

Web3 is also enabling the development of new decentralized and distributed technologies, such as blockchain, which allow for the creation of a more secure, transparent, and decentralized web. This enables the creation of new applications and services that can operate without the need for central servers or intermediaries and can provide greater control and ownership to users over their data and online experiences.

The definitions of what Web3 and/or the metaverse will actually look like and how we will operate in it are just now being defined. That's one of the most exciting elements of this time in technology history – it is wide open and ready for invention and imagination.

The rise of Web3 and NFTs was building for a few years, and by March 2021, the acceleration and visibility jumped to another level when this headline[7] appeared: "*Beeple Crypto Art Sold for $69M at Christie's Auction*". It seemed that the whole world then exclaimed, "What! $69 million dollars is an insane amount of money. What does this even mean? What is Crypto Art? Who is Beeple? Why would Christie's even be interested? Is this a joke? Isn't crypto a bad word, something linked to shady people and unsavory activities?"

This watershed moment galvanized and gave momentum to the burgeoning NFT/Web3 ecosystem and their communities. Think of it! Digital art has value. And the artist can be handsomely compensated. And the community matters.

The concept of Web3 is closely aligned with cryptocurrency, as many of the commercial transactions in the Web3 ecosystem are conducted using digital currencies. Early users of Web3 typically maintain a "crypto wallet" or "digital vault" to enable these transactions. However, as Web3 technology and the use of NFTs become more widespread, it is likely that more user-friendly and familiar payment methods will emerge, such as a "credit card-like" NFT system.

The ongoing debate about the balance between centralization and decentralization in the Web3 ecosystem will also play a role in the development and adoption of Web3 technology. Some argue that centralization can provide greater security and ease of use, while others believe that decentralization is essential to the principles of Web3 and the blockchain. Is there a middle ground or a combination of the two? That is yet to be determined.

Clearly, the rise of NFTs and Web3 technology is a significant shift that has the potential to fundamentally change the balance of power and money on the Internet. As more people and businesses become aware of the potential of NFTs to enable creators to retain ownership and control over their work and to monetize their creations, it is likely that the use of NFTs and Web3 technology will continue to grow and evolve.

Exploring New Business Models

Brands and enterprises are beginning to explore the new benefits that NFTs and Web3 might offer. New monetization opportunities, new customer engagement, and new business models are on the horizon.

Brands are learning that drafting and negotiating agreements involving NFTs require at least some understanding of the underlying technology, royalty structure, new business models, and the novel legal issues they present.

Creators are exploring monetization opportunities and increased community engagement. Prior to the advent of NFTs, creators had to navigate a complex set of gatekeepers in order to go to market. Artists needed galleries. Musicians needed record labels and streaming services. Writers needed publishers. Filmmakers needed studios and distribution.

Consumer interest is growing as well. Recent research from <u>The Harris Poll</u>[8] and R&CPMK found that about half of consumers familiar with NFTs (47%) are interested in companies offering them as a commercial product.

In addition to consumers minting NFTs as a purchase incentive or memorabilia, NFTs are also sellable and tradeable products themselves. This offers new ways for consumers to potentially generate revenue.

When a minted NFT is purchased, the owner could then have the digital rights to resell, distribute or license their asset in any way they choose, depending on the elements in the smart contract. The owner possesses a wholly unique version of the asset, but in many cases, the original piece of art, gif, tweet, or video is still available for others to see.

The value of an NFT can vary greatly based on how desirable it is. NFTs projects from celebrities, popular influencers, or those which capture a momentous occasion can be extremely valuable. Typically, this value is driven by both scarcity and rarity, which signify something unique about an NFT or an NFT collection.

NFT Benefits for Brands

NFTs offer a number of potential benefits for brands. Some of these benefits include:

- **Increased engagement**: NFTs can provide a new way for brands to interact with their customers and create more engaging experiences. For example, a brand could create a unique NFT for each customer that unlocks exclusive content or rewards.
- **Improved ownership & control**: NFTs can provide a way for brands to securely and verifiably own and control their digital assets. This can help to prevent counterfeiting and ensure that the brand's intellectual property is protected.
- **New revenue streams**: NFTs can create new opportunities for brands to monetize their digital assets and generate revenue. For example, a brand could create and sell NFTs that represent unique in-game items or other digital collectibles.
- **Enhanced trust & transparency**: NFTs can provide a transparent and auditable record of ownership and provenance. This can help to build trust with customers and other stakeholders and provide a way to verify the authenticity of a brand's products or services.

- **Increased market reach**: NFTs can expand the market for a brand's digital assets by making it easier for customers to buy and trade them. This can help to reach a wider audience and tap into new sources of demand for the brand's products or services.

Brands and their influencers are seeking to find the best way to be relevant in this new space. Most have spent the last decade building massive follower bases only to find out that the ground is shifting beneath them.

Some are worried that NFTs pose a threat to brand and influencer partnerships. It's true that NFTs are potentially disruptive, but brands that pivot and are willing to broaden their concept of providing value to their customers will adapt well.

Brands can consider extending product lines into the digital world as one possible use for NFTs. Tying NFTs to loyalty programs is another. Tying NFT 'drops' to philanthropic efforts can also enhance brand perception. In addition, brands can now track the ownership and origin of their assets and ensure that the data associated with them is accurate. Digital goods could help simplify complex supply chain and logistics issues.

Consumers demand transparency, and NFTs provide a way for brands to potentially meet this need. And finally, NFTs offer a way for brands to engage with their customers more effectively.

As an example, in May 2022, Vogue Singapore[9] partnered with five artists from The MetaArt Club. The project highlighted inclusivity, diversity, and celebrating individuality with a collaborative drop of ten pieces. These pieces are a mix of digital art, video clips, and gaming avatars – all now available on OpenSea.

Other brands, like Starbucks, are entering the market by building on already-successful loyalty programs. Starbucks Odyssey is billed as an 'experience' that combines the company's successful Starbucks Rewards loyalty program with an NFT platform, allowing its customers to both earn and purchase digital assets that unlock exclusive experiences and rewards.

Interestingly, the company touts that the new program happens to be built on blockchain and Web3 tech, but the customer will never know that. NFT and blockchain are not mentioned at all. This could well be the way of the future.

Brands can also capitalize on the revenue generation that NFTs offer by 'minting' digital assets and 'dropping' those assets, much like a music album.

In December 2021, Adidas surprised the fashion world with an NFT/metaverse announcement.[10] The sportswear giant announced its first NFT[11] drop of digital and physical goods created in collaboration with Bored Ape Yacht Club, Pixel Vault's PUNKS Comic, and crypto investor gmoney, some of the hottest names in the NFT space. The company brought in over $23 million within minutes of its drop of 30,000 NFTs.

NFT Benefits for Creators

NFTs have several potential benefits for creators, including:

- **Verification & authentication**: NFTs provide a unique, verifiable digital signature for each individual work of art or creative asset. This can help creators to prove ownership and authenticity of their work, protecting against counterfeiting and plagiarism.

- **Increased ownership & control**: With NFTs, creators have more control over their digital creations, as they can set rules and conditions for how the assets can be used and distributed. This can help creators to monetize their work more effectively and maintain control over their digital creations.

- **Increased liquidity & market exposure**: The use of NFTs can help to create a more liquid and transparent marketplace for digital art and other creative assets. This can make it easier for creators to sell their work and reach a wider audience of potential buyers.

- **Increased value**: Because NFTs are unique and scarce, they can potentially increase the value of a digital asset. This can provide a financial incentive for creators to produce high-quality work and invest in the development of their digital creations.

NFTs give creators the guarantee of ownership and financial leverage over their intellectual property and assets associated with that intellectual property. Web3 is democratizing the Internet, and now creators are potentially free from the monetization policies imposed by brands, advertisers, and gatekeepers to get compensated fairly for their work.

The gatekeeper business model has been in place for many years. With the gatekeeper often retaining up to 80% of profits earned, it's easy to understand why. If a creator strikes it big, then their 20% could be significant. If the creator is less than big, the pickings are slim. 20% of very little is very little.

The NFT ownership model radically changes the old way by ushering in a new vision for creators to monetize and engage with fans and consumers.

Instead of an artist being paid only once for the sale of their art, they can now potentially receive additional compensation every time the art is resold. This is not always a given – as the royalties part of the business model continues to be under discussion by some blockchains and collections.

As an example, a photographer whose photograph is shared 1+ million times on Instagram could finally receive compensation for their work because they own the NFT and the smart contract associated with that NFT. The smart contract contains instructions as to how the work is to be used and who should receive rights and compensation going forward.

Creators now own and control the 'master'. At the time of minting, the creator institutes a smart contract that can be programmed to govern things like royalty payments and permissions. This means that fair compensation for the artist can be programmed into the NFT that is stored on the blockchain, and that can't be changed.

NFTs could also allow fans of that artist to be a part of the success of that intellectual property in the purchase and potential resale of those tokens on secondary markets. When the art is resold, everyone potentially gets compensated again.

This represents a complete overhaul of the value-creation, and value-sharing proposition discussed earlier that has dominated the creative industries for decades. Traditionally some artists, musicians, and other creators lived in near poverty while others continued to profit from their work. The value capture proposition is finally shifting, and the creator is now in the power seat. Not the agents, not the record labels, not the publisher. This paves the way for a radical overhaul of the incentive and compensation structures currently in place.

What started with the art and collectibles world is quickly moving on to music, film, video, gaming, shopping, and rewards programs. Eventually, everything could be NFT'd - contracts, tickets, events, voting, health records, personal moments, and more.

Each creator owns their IP rights and can monetize as they wish. They can also offer licensing rights and more to holders and community members. These holders can potentially monetize on secondary markets or create new IPs.

In addition, creators no longer need 1,000,000 followers to get noticed. In the NFT world, 1,000 fans can potentially earn a creator more than they would ever see previously. Music artists claim to be making what they'd normally earn from 1 million streams in '2 minutes' with NFTs.

Community matters in Web3. This concept became very distorted in Web2 early on. 'Community' really meant consumers and potential customers to be 'targeted'. The business model of Web2 is advertiser-based. Because of that, the numbers have to be huge before they mean anything to advertisers. Millions of followers, hundreds of thousands of likes, and more somehow equaled 'engagement', which is really a misnomer. Community and community building are now at the top of the list.

Understanding the importance of community in Web3 and how to effectively engage with these new communities is critical. Those who are able to effectively navigate the dynamic world of Web3 and NFTs and their communities will be well-positioned to capitalize on the numerous opportunities that are emerging in this new field.

Building a community in the NFT space has a huge impact on the success of an NFT project, and creators are finding that a small but dedicated community can be a powerful force. This new process is not just about amassing followers but rather about fostering a passionate and engaged group of supporters who are invested in the success of the project.

NFT Benefits for Consumers

NFTs also have several potential benefits for consumers. Some of these include:

- **Verification & authentication**: NFTs provide a unique, verifiable digital signature for each individual work of art or creative asset. This can help consumers to confirm the authenticity and provenance of the assets they are purchasing, providing peace of mind and protecting against counterfeiting and fraud.
- **Increased ownership & control**: With NFTs, consumers can own a unique and verifiable digital asset rather than simply having access to a copy of the asset. This can provide a sense of ownership and control over the digital assets they purchase.
- **Increased liquidity & market exposure**: The use of NFTs can help to create a more liquid and transparent marketplace for digital art and other creative assets. This can make it easier for consumers to buy and sell the assets they own, potentially increasing their value over time.

- **Access to unique & limited-edition assets**: NFTs can provide consumers with access to unique and limited-edition digital assets that may not be available through other means. This can be particularly appealing to collectors and fans of particular artists or creators.

Clearly, art and music lovers and collectors are seeing the value of NFTs. 1-of-1 art pieces are doing quite well for both the artist and the collector, as are generative collections. New displays are coming to market, as well as cyberspaces, and the excitement around digital art for art's sake is very robust. A new 'digital collector' class is emerging as well.

For certain collectors, NFTs as commemorative memorabilia can deepen connections to a consumer's favorite sports team or musical artist, etc. This expands the ability for the fan to take something home with them from a memorable event and increases the emotional bond. It also designates the fan as a member of a larger community of like-minded people.

That *community* is a benefit for the consumer cannot be understated. The concept of belonging to a tribe is both ancient and also incredibly relevant now. Shared memories still prove to be a powerful common bond. In event management, companies like Live Nation see NFTs as a major future-looking strategy[12] for the company's concerts and events. The CEO was recently quoted as saying, "We envision Live Nation participating within the [NFT] marketplace by looking at some of our concert moments as magic moments that we could mint and attach to our ongoing ticketed festivals."

Incentive-based NFTs can prove the authenticity of a luxury item by tying a unique token to a physical product or experience to mark that purchase as special and authentic. For example, in August 2022, Tiffany & Co[13] debuted and quickly sold out a limited collection of 250 custom jewel-encrusted pendants for holders of CryptoPunks, a popular early NFT collection. Over $50 million in revenue was generated.

Consumers can also resell NFTs on the secondary market if they wish. In a radical turn of events, Yuga Labs, the founding company of the Bored Ape Yacht Club[14] (BAYC) NFT collection and also specific CryptoPunks, offered their NFT owners the ability to exploit the IP rights to their characters commercially. This. Is. Critical. The IP rights go to YOU, the holder, to do with as you wish.

NFT Benefits for Enterprises

NFTs allow data to be containerized into shareable, tradeable, and trackable assets. Once data is containerized as an NFT, enterprises can share these NFTs as an asset amongst themselves.

When data is converted into an NFT, its creation, modification, sharing, and consent can all be recorded, thus creating a verifiable audit trail that enables enterprises to comply with relevant regulations. Here are potential uses for NFTs in the Enterprise:

- **Digital art & collectibles**: NFTs can be used to authenticate and verify the ownership of digital art and collectibles. This can create a new market for artists and collectors and provide a way for them to sell and trade their digital creations.
- **Gaming**: NFTs can be used to represent unique in-game items, such as weapons, armor, or virtual real estate. This can provide a way for players to own and

trade these items and create new revenue streams for game developers. Gamification can also be added to loyalty programs, etc.

- **Supply chain tracking**: NFTs can be used to track the movement of goods and materials through the supply chain. This can provide a tamper-proof record of the history and provenance of a product and help to ensure its quality and authenticity.
- **Identity verification**: NFTs can be used to verify the identity of individuals and organizations. This can provide a secure and verifiable way to establish and maintain trust online.
- **Real estate**: NFTs can be used to represent ownership of physical assets, such as real estate or cars. This can provide a convenient and secure way to transfer ownership and manage these assets.
- **Tickets & passes**: NFTs can be used to represent tickets and passes to events and services. This can provide a convenient and secure way to manage access and reduce the risk of counterfeiting.
- **Digital content**: NFTs can be used to represent and protect digital content, such as music, videos, or books. This can provide a way for creators to monetize their content and control its distribution.
- **Loyalty & rewards programs**: NFTs can be used to represent rewards and points in loyalty and rewards programs. This can provide a way for businesses to offer and manage incentives for their customers.
- **Voting & governance**: NFTs can be used to represent and manage votes and other forms of participation in governance processes. This can provide a secure and

transparent way to conduct elections and other decision-making processes.

- **Fundraising & investment**: NFTs can be used to represent ownership stakes in businesses and other ventures. This can provide a way for companies to raise capital and for investors to participate in these opportunities.

Expanding on the example in the area of real estate, the concept of transacting with the use of a verified NFT of a physical property through the blockchain is gaining traction. In June 2022, this headline[15] appeared: "$26.5M NYC Building Listed on OpenSea". "Yes. You get the property after buying the NFT," the owner tweeted in response to those who thought it was some kind of scam. "Yes, you can live in the building. Yes, you can rent it out. It's not just an expensive jpeg." Some call this the future of real estate.

NFTs can be used to represent ownership of real-world property. Currently, deeds serve this function, and buyers employ title insurance companies, escrow holders, and lawyers to authenticate deeds and search for encumbrances in public title records. NFTs could provide a way to potentially bypass trusted intermediaries because blockchains can verify ownership, identify title encumbrances and settle transactions more efficiently.

Metaverse platforms like Decentraland and Sandbox sell parcels of digital land by associating each parcel with an NFT and recording transactions on blockchains like Ethereum. After a buyer purchases a virtual parcel, the transaction is recorded on the blockchain, and the NFT is transferred to the buyer's digital wallet.

Metaverse platforms can then authenticate land parcel ownership when a user links a wallet to the platform. Users can also participate in governance if the platform is operated as a decentralized autonomous organization (or DAO) that allows token holders to vote on initiatives.

NFT Benefits for B2B Startups

The Web3 and NFT space is ripe with potential for new business opportunities in the business-to-business category. Companies that can provide the necessary infrastructure, marketplaces, and community-building tools for Web3 can help to drive the growth of this exciting new market and create new revenue streams for themselves.

One of the biggest opportunities in this space is the development of infrastructure that can support the growing demand for decentralized applications (dApps) and (NFTs). This includes things like blockchain networks, smart contract platforms, and other technologies that are needed to support these new forms of online activity.

Another area of opportunity is the development of marketplaces for buying and selling NFTs. With the popularity of NFTs growing, there is a need for online platforms where people can easily buy and sell these unique digital assets. Companies that can provide reliable and user-friendly marketplaces can tap into this demand and create new revenue streams.

In addition to infrastructure and marketplaces, there are also opportunities for companies to create software and tools that can help facilitate community building and relationship management within the Web3 and NFT space. This can include things like social networking platforms,

forms, and other online tools that can help people connect with each other and build strong communities around their shared interests.

Companies like Dust Labs, for instance, are building B2B software for Web3 communities, starting with NFTs and brands. The technology they are developing has been used to build the two popular NFT collections – DeGods and y00ts.

Current NFT Categories

It is important to acknowledge that NFT categories will continue to expand as new innovations come to market.

NFT as Profile Picture (PFP) or Avatar

NFTs have gained popularity as profile pictures or avatars on social media platforms. One of the first examples of this is the "CryptoPunks" created by Larva Lab founders Matt Hall and John Watkinson in 2017. These avatars were generated and distributed for free on the Ethereum blockchain and were initially seen as collectibles. As their value increased, users began to utilize them as profile pictures on social media, indicating their involvement in the CryptoPunk community. In May 2021, a <u>Christie's auction</u>[16] sold nine CryptoPunk portraits for nearly $17 million, highlighting the value and popularity of these NFTs as profile pictures.

NFT as Generative Art

Generative art is a form of art that is created using a computer and often involves the use of generative algorithms or artificial intelligence. It is a type of collaborative art where the artist works with an autonomous system to create unique pieces. The use of NFTs in generative art allows for the creation of truly unique and rare pieces, as the parameters included in the NFT are always different. This allows for the creation of digital scarcity and the ability to easily trade and exchange these art pieces. The use of NFTs in generative art also allows for the artist to retain ownership and control over their work.

NFT 1-of-1 Artwork

1-of-1 art refers to a unique NFT that represents a single piece of art. This scarcity creates a higher value for the art piece, as there is only one in existence. Artists such as Beeple, XCOPY, and Pak have achieved great success and realized millions from the sale of their 1-of-1 NFTs. 1-of-1 art can also refer to a physical piece of art or another asset that has a digital twin in the form of an NFT. This allows for the creation of a digital presence for the physical asset, enabling it to be easily traded and exchanged using blockchain technology.

NFT as Collectible

NFTs can also be used as collectibles, which are minted on NFT marketplaces. These platforms, built on Web3 blockchain technology, allow for the creation and trading of NFTs with other users. Collectible NFTs are valued based on their scarcity and demand among collectors.

NFTs as collectibles can represent a wide range of digital assets, including in-game items or skins, digital representations of physical items, and more. They can also be traded, allowing collectors to easily buy and sell their collections.

One example of an NFT collectible ecosystem is NBA Top Shot, which focuses solely on the NBA, its players, and "moments" from the game. Another example is the recently announced MLB NFT offering, called Candy, for fans of major league baseball.

The use of NFTs as collectibles provides a clear transaction history and provenance for the item, which can help to combat counterfeiting. This added layer of security and authenticity makes NFT collectibles an attractive option for both casual and serious collectors.

NFTs with Utility

NFTs with "utility" are those that are assigned a specific use or permission beyond just ownership of the associated digital or physical asset. These NFTs provide added value for investors, artists, gamers, and brands.

Utility NFTs have clearly defined intrinsic value beyond their scarcity. For example, holding a token could grant access to exclusive experiences, early access to products, entry to members-only virtual and physical events, or dividends. The possibilities for utility NFTs are vast, and creators with a strategic mindset and vision can take advantage of this growing market.

Utility NFTs are creating new business opportunities that did not previously exist. They enable token holders to unlock special privileges or access to events and sales. Artists can attach instructions to an NFT to ensure they receive royalty payments every time it is resold, allowing them to benefit from the increase in value of their work. NFTs can also provide musicians with the ability to offer unique media and perks to their fans. Overall, utility NFTs are expanding the possibilities for digital assets and creating new ways for individuals and businesses to interact and engage with one another.

Gamified NFTs

Gamification can apply to 'regular' NFTs specifically, as well as to blockchain-based games in general. Gamification is not new. In fact, we discussed it at length in *The Power of Real-Time Social Media Marketing*,[17] published in 2011. It's gotten much more sophisticated since then.

Gamified NFTs incorporate elements of gamification, which involves using incentives to reward certain behaviors. Gamers are already familiar with gamified incentives, such as gated rewards, and the combination of gaming, NFT technology, and cryptocurrency is expected to power the growth of the metaverse and Web3.

Gamification can also be seen in more simplified forms, such as airline rewards miles or buy one, get one free (BOGO) offers. Many brands are looking to incorporate NFTs into their customer loyalty programs, with companies like Starbucks and Bud Light announcing new membership programs on a regular basis. Gamified NFTs provide an engaging and rewarding experience for consumers and offer new opportunities for brands to connect with their customers.

NFTs as Tickets

Beyond art, photography, music, and other digital assets, event tickets have become a way for event holders to utilize the blockchain and NFTs. NFT ticketing enables holders to use tokens as an access pass for live or virtual events.

NFTs provide a secure and verifiable way for event organizers to manage ticket sales and ensure that only legitimate ticket holders are able to access the event. This can help to reduce the risk of counterfeiting and scalping, as well as provide a better experience for fans by allowing them to easily transfer their tickets to friends or resell them on the secondary market. Additionally, the use of NFTs allows event organizers to track and analyze ticket sales data in real time, which can be used to optimize pricing and marketing strategies.

This is an intriguing new way to maintain a deeper relationship with fans and a way to offer surprise perks or set up exclusive privileges for fans.

NFT Communities

NFT communities are groups of individuals who are interested in the NFT space and are looking to engage with other creators and fans of NFTs. These communities often form around specific projects or creators and can provide valuable support and engagement for each other.

One of the key benefits of NFT communities is that they provide a platform for creators to share their work and receive feedback from other members of the community. This can be incredibly valuable for creators, as it can help them to improve their work and create more compelling NFTs. Communities can also provide a way for creators to promote their work and connect with new audiences, which can lead to increased demand for their NFTs.

In addition to providing support for creators, NFT communities can also be a great way for individuals to learn more about the NFT space and connect with like-minded individuals. Many communities have dedicated forums, Discord channels, and social media groups where members can discuss NFTs, share their own projects, and learn from others in the community.

Building a community is not easy, nor is it a new concept. The NFT space itself is a community. People invest time in it, sharing ideas, collaborating, talking on Twitter Spaces, and also supporting and buying into each other's art and projects.

NFT communities play a crucial role in the success of the NFT space. By providing support and engagement for creators and fans alike, these communities help to drive the growth and development of the NFT market and pave the way for the future of digital ownership.

Importance of Value in NFTs

Value is a bit like beauty. They say, "Beauty is in the eye of the beholder". *Value* is in the eye of the beholder as well. Value is what you say it is. Value is what 'they' say it is. The market determines value.

Brands talk about core values, mission, and vision. People assign value to what matters to them. Value in terms of commerce is 'whatever the market will bear'.

Like Value, the concept and definition of beauty has literally been debated for thousands of years. Who determines what is truly beautiful? As far back as Homer's *The Iliad*, Helen of Troy was considered so beautiful that her 'face launched a thousand ships'. Even today, people will ask, "Is Mona Lisa really beautiful?"

During the historical Renaissance, beauty was debated constantly. The art patrons – those nobles and princes who were financed by the bankers - often dictated what was considered beauty.

In our times, it is the concept of Value that is at the forefront of the NFT renaissance. In business and in real life (IRL), we often talk about value - adding value, value propositions, and considering the value of an asset, a company, or a new product. What is value, and what creates value? What makes something valuable? Who establishes value? Is value only financial? What other types of value can be created? Is there really value in an NFT or any digital asset, for that matter?

In the NFT world, a new type of value is attached to uniquely identifiable digital assets. In addition to the traditional elements of what constitutes value, the market is now able to establish the *value and ownership* of these identifiable digital assets as a cryptographic verification on the blockchain. This Certificate of Authenticity becomes the asset's *provenance.*

NFT Provenance

Provenance is one of the backbones of all economies, whether it relates to artifacts, real estate, gems, etc. There has always been a need to authenticate that a party actually owns an asset prior to any business deals involving that asset to ensure that the asset is "true" rather than stolen or faked.

Provenance is not a new concept by any means. The term dates back to the 1780s in the English language. It has fueled the luxury and high-market auction houses for many years. Documenting the provenance of a given item (painting, jewelry, auto, etc.) is part of the trade. In fact, sometimes tracing provenance is quite literally an art form in and of itself.

Provenance, as defined by the Oxford English Dictionary, is "a record of ownership of a work of art or an antique, used as a guide to authenticity or quality." As such, provenance could be further defined as an immutable audit archive of ownership.

In fact, many industries still use paper to prove whether something is real or whether a particular person actually owns an asset. Paper can be altered or lost. In the purchase of high-value assets, it is easy for the corresponding certificate to say one thing but for the asset to be something entirely different.

Today, rather than relying on "trusted" third parties who have traditionally played this role, the possibility exists for blockchain technology to streamline this function by serving as the infrastructure for registering and authenticating asset ownership between all parties with common interests.

Therefore, Blockchain technology can ensure provenance by enforcing transparency, authenticity, security, and auditability of an asset's digital twin. *Digital Provenance,* then, is metadata that establishes the chain-of-custody information that authenticates ownership. Today known as 'cryptographic verification'.

As the current NFT tsunami wave continues to grow and provenance is now 'provable' via the blockchain, it is dawning on many that owning and claiming one's own IP and incenting a community of fans and admirers to share in projects is a massive consumer and audience shift that has only just begun. This shift will change the balance of attention, money, and influence on the Internet forever.

It still remains to be seen who actually enforces this Certificate of Authentication should there be a dispute. There is also a myriad of copyright issues that have plagued the art and music industries going back many years, and NFTs might only add a layer of complexity to an already complex subject. Just look at the recent announcement that Miramax is suing Quentin Tarantino for his foray into NFTs with Pulp Fiction. They finally came to an agreement, but the waters are still muddy. Not to mention how the financial gains or losses might be dealt with as it relates to tax policy and more.

These very important considerations need to be addressed in this new frontier. And they will be. Smart lawyers, accountants, policy wonks, and more are already hard at work figuring this out.

Don't forget, at the advent of the Internet in the dot-com era, these same concerns emerged and subsequently got worked out, for the most part. Digital law and digital finance are often slow to catch up to technology, but perhaps this current digital onslaught will force renewed attention and help accelerate the process.

Conclusion

What does all this mean? Simply put: A New Renaissance in creativity that includes Ownership and Control is well underway. We are now talking about something of value that you own the rights to, that can be verified on an immutable record, and can then be bought, sold, and/or traded at the owner's discretion.

It is understandable that this sea-change in how the Internet, information, money, ownership, and creativity might seem baffling. A new level of understanding regarding the true value and who 'owns' that value is at the core of this discussion.

The Use Cases detailed in Chapter 4 are an excellent example of how NFTs are rapidly spreading to new domains and industries, and creativity seems to know no bounds. They cover iconic brands as well as NFT-native brands and provide eye-opening insights into how NFTs are already being deployed.

NFTs and Web3 technology are revolutionizing the way that creators can establish the value of their work and monetize it. This is particularly exciting for artists and other creatives who have traditionally struggled to make a living from their work. With the rise of NFTs, creators are establishing the value of their creations and receiving royalties on their work, even after it has been sold. This has led to the growth of vibrant culture and the emergence of new communities of artists, musicians, and all content creators who are using the internet to share their work and connect with audiences.

Challenges Ahead

As the NFT and Web3 industries continue to grow, they are accompanied by challenges that must be addressed in order to sustain and further develop these technologies. Some of these challenges include the high energy consumption associated with blockchain technology, the lack of regulatory frameworks for NFTs, and the need for better user education and awareness about the potential uses and limitations of NFTs.

Additionally, the potential for fraud and scams within the NFT space is a concern, as is the issue of interoperability between different blockchain networks and NFT standards. Security, privacy, sustainability, and scalability – all pose challenges going forward. It will be important for industry leaders and stakeholders to work together to address these challenges and continue to push the boundaries of what is possible with NFTs and Web3 technology.

The future of the NFT space is bright. As the technology continues to evolve and more creators and businesses adopt NFTs, we can expect to see new applications and use cases emerge, as well as new opportunities for creators to thrive in the digital world. However, it is important for creators, investors, and consumers to be aware of the potential challenges and pitfalls associated with this technology and to approach the NFT market with caution.

Developments to Watch For:

- **Scalability:** Scalability must improve for widespread adoption. This refers to the ability of a network to handle a large number of transactions per second (TPS) without compromising its security or effectiveness.
- **Interoperability:** New thinking on the interoperability of blockchains is needed. As the bear market of 2022 continued, blockchain experts were calling for a new standard of interoperability after a series of record-breaking crypto hacks, and bridge exploits hurt the industry.

- **Business to Business**: Web3 B2B tools for onboarding, usability, customer relationships, community management, content creation and distribution, and much more will be a growth area going forward.
- **Upgradable Smart Contracts**: Blockchains are meant to be immutable, and the data stored on the Ethereum blockchain, which includes the smart contracts deployed to it, is also immutable. However, upgradable smart contracts should be considered to fix bugs, improve functionality, optimize code, etc.
- **Loyalty Programs**: There is already massive interest from brands eyeing NFT-based customer loyalty programs going into the near future. Seeing luxury brands using NFTs to enable access to exclusive customer experiences and perks is definitely appealing and will continue to grow.
- **Social Media**: The popularity of NFTs in social media is exploding. Avatars and virtual identities will build on social credibility on platforms like TikTok, Instagram, Twitter, etc.
- **New Applications**: Gaming, Music, Ticketing, Identity dApps, Retail, Fashion - these new applications for NFTs will permit musicians, designers, and more to incorporate explicit terms and rules into their smart contract agreements, which can incorporate admittance to particular occasions, and digital or IRL asset deliveries. This not only enables new associations with fans and customers but also creates wholly new revenue streams.
- **FUN!** Creating something new is fun. It's inspiring to see new groups of people forming around their

interests and businesses with renewed energy and excitement. We will not be abandoning Web2 any time soon. This is not an end but another beginning. And it's one you do not want to miss!

Chapter 2

The Arc from PCs to NFTs

From Corporate America to entrepreneur to the academic world, my vantage points have enabled a unique set of perspectives on major developments over the years. This has made me especially qualified to frame these new tectonic developments with both an eye to the future and relevant context from my own emerging technology journey.

When *The Power of Real-Time Social Media Marketing* was published, the potential value of social media and its relevance was hard for many to grasp at first. I understood it and could translate its meaning to businesses, students, and brands. I traveled to boardrooms and executive meetings all around the world to help foster critical thinking among decision-makers and leaders around these new developments.

The context for WHY the current changes are meaningful is important. It is one thing to say, "NFTs! The new, shiny object everyone should pay attention to." Or "This (fill in the blank) will change the world as we know it!" Really? And why is that? It might sound good, but it could very well be empty platitudes. The true meaning and business value are more complex and nuanced.

I was just starting out as a professional in the early 1980s when the technological changes of the day would prove as revolutionary in its time as the Internet was 20 years later and NFTs and Web3 promise to be today.

From MS-DOS and the first Personal Computers (PCs) to the Apple Macintosh, from the first GPS satellites to Tim Berners-Lee, Godfather of the early Internet, at CERN Switzerland – 1980 was an amazing time to be starting out in what was then called 'high-tech'.

I was a young computer programmer back then, at the very beginning of my career. We were called Systems Analysts in those days – today, the title would be Software Engineer. Most programmers worked for IBM, programming super-large mainframe computers that processed huge amounts of data for things like payroll and accounting.

I wasn't trained to be a programmer. I studied English Literature. A friend of mine had just purchased a mini-computer for his company in San Francisco. I visited his office one day and walked by the room where his brand-new mini-computer was located.

There was green glowing type on the screen that I later learned was 'code' or computer language. Somehow, I knew what it meant. I don't know why or how, but I did. Kind of like those who pick up languages or can play music, just like that.

I learned to program that computer for him from the manual (no help from Google or YouTube in those days!) and went on to learn early programming languages like BASIC (Beginners' All-purpose Symbolic Instruction Code) and COBOL (Common Business Oriented Language). COBOL is still used today in places like government and banking. Believe it or not, an estimated 43% of banking systems and 95% of ATM swipes still utilize COBOL codes. That's either scary or amazing, depending on how you look at it.

My world was mainframe and mini-computers from then on, and our crowd paid little attention to much else in the tech world. America was still basking in the glow of the moon landing. Millions of people around the world had gathered around their televisions to watch two U.S. astronauts do something no one had ever done before, and computers played a big part in that. It was thrilling to be in the field.

Game giant Atari was founded in 1972 with its famous "Pong" game. By the early 80s, Atari was selling at-home game consoles. The Altair personal computer was introduced in 1974 and was sold at Radio Shack stores. It was interesting because it had the Intel chip in it. Intel was a big deal in "the Valley" (not yet 'Silicon Valley') in those days – one of the legacy startup stories that has been told time and again. Intel was founded in Mountain View, California, in 1968 by Gordon E. Moore (known for the famous "Moore's law" of diminishing returns), a chemist, and Robert Noyce, a physicist and co-inventor of the integrated circuit. Arthur Rock (investor and venture capitalist) helped them find investors.

The Altair didn't go anywhere because there really wasn't a market for it yet. It was mostly for hobbyists who liked to take things apart and put them back together. But it was an early entry to the microcomputer revolution that soon dominated everything.

The Apple II was announced in 1977, but hardly anyone except tech geeks paid attention to Apple back then. It should be noted, though, that just like Tesla today, the Apple I was considered a masterpiece of design, using far fewer parts than anything in its class and quickly earning Steve Wozniak (the co-founder along with Steve Jobs) the reputation as a master designer. Of course, Steve Jobs also rose to legendary status for many reasons later on, mostly all well-deserved.

The cascade of these products – Atari, Altair, Apple – was a precursor to the formula that would drive innovation in Silicon Valley for decades. Those who were all about making things possible that had never been possible before using leading-edge technology and plenty of capital would almost always win the race.

The IBM PC/XT was announced in 1981, and the first Apple Macintosh in 1984. The marketing for that first Mac is legendary even today. At the time, most tech companies didn't advertise and, in fact, thought that if you *had* to advertise, you were doing something wrong. The only place you might advertise would be business magazines or televised U.S. Open golf tournaments. Too many ads were for losers in those days.

Apple did its share of business advertising like everyone else. The infamous Chiat\Day[18] advertising agency was Apple's AOR (agency of record). For the rollout of the Macintosh, Apple's personal computer, Apple wanted to do something truly groundbreaking. Their revolutionary idea was to produce an ad for the upcoming Super Bowl that would get attention. Their biggest competitor was IBM at the time, and IBM owned the PC market, such as it was. IBM rarely advertised and certainly not on television. And most certainly not during the Super Bowl!

Steve Jobs came up with an iconic and historic advertising campaign that is the now infamous Apple Macintosh 1984 commercial[19] and announcement. Ridley Scott[20], the famous movie director (Alien, Blade Runner), was the director of the advertisement.

It was inspired by George Orwell's novel 1984 and depicted a dystopian future in which a totalitarian government controls its citizens through the use of propaganda and technology. In the ad, a young woman representing the Mac throws a sledgehammer at a large screen displaying the image of the government's leader, symbolizing the power of the Mac to challenge authority and break through the limitations of traditional computing.

I make sure all students who have taken my classes at UCLA see this commercial, and we use it as a case study both in marketing and technology and business change management.

To say this was a groundbreaking event is an understatement. In those days, the 1980s and into the 1990s, most commercials that aired during sports broadcasts were centered on beer, cars, and girls. It was *definitely* a different time.

But Apple has always seemed to have the ability to create a vision for consumers of what new technology would enable them to do and why it would be meaningful to them. When that 1984 Macintosh commercial came on the air, it got everyone's attention, some good, some not-so-good, some tongue-in-cheek. The Apple Board apparently hated it. Others deemed it 'the best science fiction movie trailer they had ever seen'.

That "1984" ad ran in its full 60-second length only once on national television — during the third quarter of Super Bowl XVIII on January 22, 1984. It cost $500,000 at the time, and Chiat\Day[21] estimated that Apple received roughly $45 million of free advertising from TV stations covering it. Talk about return on investment!

The marketing lesson was clear - get everyone talking about your new ad instead of the big game. Who was the winning team that year, anyway? Oh, right, the San Francisco 49ers. 1984 was a great year for the Bay Area!

During those early years, I realized I was learning something very valuable – both from my work at Wang Labs and from bold statements from companies like Apple. The market sends signals that can be read if you know where to look and how to process the information. I was good at that. Innovation is disruptive because most people don't get it at first.

Not everyone is a visionary, but those who truly are become the arbiters of change and hopefully change for good. The ability to spot that and then leverage that for your business and/or customers is a winning ticket every time.

I quickly moved from the mini and mainframe world to the world of the connected computer via networking and associated software development. I loved my years at Xerox Corporation, starting as a Systems Analyst working with the Xerox STAR[22] system (by then the ViewPoint). It was a heady time. Xerox PARC (Palo Alto Research Center) was inventing like crazy – the mouse, laser printing, and much more. Just ask Apple, who, they say, poached many Xerox PARC engineers[23] in those early years. But that's another story for someone else to tell.

Mostly, I learned about strategy and the importance of implementing a good sales and customer service process during that time. Those were the great days of Corporate America when employees were well-valued and given good training in leadership, quality management, and more.

My number one takeaway from those early years was to always be curious and keep watching how the market adopted and adapted to new changes. Was this truly a change that would affect business or simply a passing fad or a piece of technology that was a solution looking for a problem? I kept moving to the latest 'new thing' in computers and technology, and I was right – that time turned out to be just about the biggest change ever. Your laptop, tablet, and smartphone all these years later prove it.

I also kept a keen eye on how these companies sold and marketed their products. If really smart people barely understood what was happening or hardly had the vision to see what *might* happen, how could the average consumer or businessperson be expected to get it? How does a company educate while at the same time market the product? Who's doing it well, and who is failing? Sounds a lot like our current time with NFTs and Web3, doesn't it?

The NFT space has literally exploded since March 2020. It contains everything I am passionate about – emerging tech, smart people, and brands jumping in, redefining money and value, the metaverse, and new forms of commerce – I just can't resist. Where will all this lead? The journey continues.

I watched the significant uptick in the rise of NFTs and Web3 concepts from 2020 – 2021 during the pandemic, which offered the time and space for many people to re-assess and re-evaluate their work and lifestyle choices. As the NFT and Web3 space emerged, I realized it was offering one of the most exciting developments in the last 20+ years. That says a lot.

It is folly to think you know everything about a subject, and those that do are boring and glum. My hashtag back in the early days of Web2 was #AlwaysBeLearning. Being curious and always learning has held me in good stead my whole life. Employers today look for candidates who are curious. Why? Because today's workforce must remain dynamic and teachable in order to keep up. Plus, it's fun to be curious and always be learning. It makes life full and interesting and is great for mental health.

I love strategy and thinking strategically. I always include lectures about strategy in the courses I teach at UCLAx and UCLA Anderson School of Management. I am a Strategic Advisor to clients. I have helped executives I have coached over the years to think more strategically. Strategy is about vision and mapping from here to there. Tactics are about execution and day-to-day next steps. Both are critically important and often dismissed as 'nice to have' instead of foundational.

I watch trends and brands and new technology and ask, "WHY is this happening? What is the strategic motivation behind the recent ad campaign or new product?" Corporate America and multinational companies don't do things on a whim. There is planning and research informing their market moves. That planning and research inform strategy.

I take students through these exercises – if a brand is succeeding or failing, we turn it into a case study to find out WHY. What brought them to this point, how is the competition reacting, and what do we think will happen next?

Will Web3 and NFTs specifically be any different? We don't know the end of this story yet, and things can and will go terribly wrong for some projects. There is always the threat of risk in any business venture. There will be bear markets, and there will be bull markets - that much doesn't change. There will be 'rug pulls' as the bottom of a project drops out.

We are also facing massive unknowns – like artificial intelligence for the masses, shifts in geopolitics, global macroeconomics, space exploration, population fluctuations, and so much more.

Yes, there are bad actors in the NFT space and on the Internet in general. Just think of all the data breaches, identity theft, and misinformation campaigns that make the news practically every day. There were downfalls and detractors with the IBM PC; the early dot-com days (just remember the million dollar sock pet puppet from the massive Pets.com fail[24]); early social media; and now with Web3 and NFTs.

There will be downturns in this new Web3 age, and there will be scams. If we've learned anything about the Internet over the past 20 years, it's that scammers are out there, they are automated, and there will be those who will fall prey. Unfortunately, the eye-popping sticker prices of some NFT sales making headlines have become a main attraction for bad actors.

Many will want to equate the current NFT craze with the Dutch Tulip Mania[25] of the 1600s or to the "Beanie Babies"[26] fad of a number of years ago. You can search online for both, but here's the bottom line: At one point in a consumer craze, the bottom dropped out, and many were left with products that were seemingly worthless.

By the late 1990s, "Beanie Babies", a $5 toy shipped from China, became such a big craze that people - mostly adults - paid thousands of dollars to collect them. But only a few years after Beanie Babies made their creator a billionaire, the stuffed animals became virtually worthless. Some got rich, but most were left high and dry. There were even stories of garages filled with the worthless toy after the bottom dropped out. A true rug pull, for sure.

On the other hand, the promise of the NFT and smart contracts, ownership, and empowering the creator economy is certainly compelling. It is attracting a new group of entrepreneurs as well as iconic brands seeking new horizons.

In 2017, an exciting new technology was taking center stage in my world. Blockchain seemed to be everywhere. That and cryptocurrency, Bitcoin, to be exact, with Ethereum as a close runner-up. Combined with AI (Artificial Intelligence) and IOT (Internet of Things), blockchain was getting a nod from the industry as a potential new technology to take a look at.

I became an academic advisor to the student-led UCLA 'blockchain lab' with various groups meeting in small clusters around campus to explore these new ideas. I met some wonderful alumni and students involved in various projects. I also assisted Alex Nascimento, a DeFi expert and Instructor colleague of mine, in developing the curriculum for the Blockchain Certificate program for UCLA Extension. That certificate program is still going on today.

Lamborghini invited me to give a presentation to the Executive Board in Italy on Blockchain in the Enterprise in early 2018. I enlisted the LA Blockchain Lab to assist in the project. It was quite successful, and we subsequently produced a Proof of Concept that informed a partnership with Salesforce to put a 1-of-1 legacy Lamborghini vehicle on the blockchain. We made history.[27]

We were way ahead of the market. In addition to the partnership with Salesforce, we also reported on the concept of the 'tokenization of assets', i.e., tokenizing an exotic car.

Think of that – kind of the predecessor to NFTs in some ways, right? We also were careful to differentiate cryptocurrency from blockchain because, at that time, crypto was undergoing a significant PR problem. It was still deeply associated with the dark web, illegal activities, and money laundering. Plus, the ICO (Initial Coin Offering) market had just crashed the year before, and many hands got slapped by governmental agencies in the process.

Then the pandemic. Everything seemingly came to a halt – globally – by the end of March 2020. A year later, it seemed that everyone had been turning to their screens in one form or another.

Suddenly, something called an NFT, or non-fungible token, was making news. NFTs were not new, actually, but the buzz was building around March 2021. It seemed that a new way to combine cryptocurrency (at that time ETH or Ethereum) and digital assets (like CryptoKitties), governed by a 'smart contract', was suddenly sparking everyone's imagination and thinking.

Here was a new way for artists (and other creators) to go directly to the art buyer with a digital representation and/or asset and command real life-changing money, in some cases. Auction houses like Christie's and Sotheby's were involved. Soon celebrities and well-known names seemed to be speaking about NFTs. Social audio platforms like Clubhouse and Twitter Spaces were becoming virtual meeting places for everyone to gather around, offer support to one another, and learn more about just what all of this meant and how one could get involved. Something was brewing. Something disruptive and new and exciting.

I stayed in Corporate America until the dot-com craze hit in the late 1990s, and my curiosity bubbled over. I just had to go and be a part of the Internet wave. Another cutting-edge moment in history where everything changed practically overnight.

Many have written a detailed history of the technology of the Internet. What matters in my journey is that this was yet another time where the vision of the future was greater than the capacity for others to see it in the present. And the unintended benefits and pitfalls were also somewhat of a mystery to many. It can take time for the vision to become evident.

Everyone was asking, "What is the Internet? Where is it? Who owns it? And what is dot-com? No, I will never put my credit card online – I don't even use email." Can you believe that in those days, executives still printed out their emails (and faxes) to 'have a legitimate copy'? And now we have a generation who don't even know what a fax machine is! Fact.

The dot-com bubble and bust cycle are legendary. There were some very heady days back then as companies were literally created and funded – to the tune of millions – on the backs of napkins during happy hour in swanky bars or hip restaurants. The infrastructure startup I joined then ended up as part of the security and storage giant Akamai Technologies. We all did quite well in that acquisition.

Then I was on to another startup focused on media and entertainment that really did raise millions based on a 'back of the envelope' calculation. I was brought on as the Chief Marketing Officer, and we made significant headway in the space until the bubble suddenly burst in April 2001. It was like musical chairs, and some of the chairs were missing. It all came to a grinding halt. When 9-11 happened, it seemed like the whole world stopped dead in its tracks.

I started a traditional management consulting company after the dot-com crash at the end of 2001 with a business partner from Harvard Business School via Wall Street. We focused on the entertainment, healthcare, and energy industries.

Everyone was pretty gun-shy after the bottom of the dot-com market fell out, so we focused our company on traditional strategic advisory work. But emerging technology wasn't far away – our first customer was Boeing's Digital Cinema division. Way before its time, it was yet another exercise in trying to help explain the vision of the future to those who couldn't see it at the time. Of course, now, all the films you see in movie theaters are digital, but at that time, reels of 35mm films were still being shipped around the country and around the world to be shown in theaters. Today movies are all streamed via satellite (hence the involvement of Boeing).

By the summer of 2006, we were conducting leading-edge business intelligence research and analytics in the industries we focused on. One of my favorite clients was a very large managed healthcare company. The Chief Medical Officer was our primary contact – a real renaissance man, unusual for the healthcare industry. One day he asked me, "Beverly, should we be blogging?" Great question! Remember, it's 2006. At that time, you still had to explain to executives that 'blogging' meant web-log. We agreed that we would look into it on their behalf.

Blogging was gaining traction. YouTube was bought by Google in October 2006. The Apple iPod was introduced in 2003 (1,000 songs in your pocket), and there was buzz that Apple was going to introduce something truly revolutionary soon (which turned out to be the iPhone).

Lo and behold, our research on behalf of our client opened a whole world of innovation that was quietly happening just beneath the surface. We discovered the very early inklings of social media entering the business community via blogs and podcasts. Early content marketing! On the consumer side, Myspace launched in 2003, and Friendster launched the year before. Clearly, something was changing again. I am grateful to the wonderful innovator and public health advocate, <u>Dr. Sam Ho</u>[28], Chief Medical Officer at PacifiCare/United Healthcare, who later became a Board Member at Tufts University, Tufts University School of Medicine:

"I've worked with Beverly Macy over the years, and she has always been able to provide innovative strategies and programs based on relevant and comprehensive market research---many of which utilize web-based technology. Also, she has presented different intriguing ideas using cellphone technology and customized messaging, potential sensor applications within cellphones, and, most recently, extending the Internet to include podcasting and blogging as education and marketing tools." Thank you, Dr. Ho!

I helped launch a medical and health radio channel on Sirius/XM Radio in 2008 with a wonderful team. That was fun, as satellite radio was just beginning to get big. This was a novel concept, as at the time, satellite radio subscriptions were just starting to gain popularity among consumers and be included with new car sales. With the success of personalities like Howard Stern leaving terrestrial (AM/FM) radio and the growing popularity of satellite radio, the idea of a medical radio channel created and run by doctors was a unique and forward-thinking approach. It was well ahead of the market trends, again showcasing my ability to identify and capitalize on emerging opportunities in the industry.

At that time, I was also teaching marketing at UCLA Extension. I felt compelled to give back to the next generation what had been given to me in terms of industry and marketing knowledge. I approached the Dean of UCLA Extension and suggested we develop a marketing class introducing students to this brand new development, social media.

In August of 2007, I unveiled a curriculum I developed for UCLA Extension for a one-day seminar I gave along with a fellow Instructor, Karl Kasca. It was entitled: Social Media 101 *Podcasts, YouTube, and Blogs — What They Are and How Corporations Can Use Them.*

We arrived very early in the morning to set up. It was a Saturday seminar, and it was already a hot summer day in Southern California. There was a line of people along the side of the building, which was not unusual because there were always a number of events going on around the UCLA campus.

It turned out this line – at 7:30 AM on that hot summer morning – was for the Social Media seminar. Wow. What a site. We had over 100+ people crammed into a classroom in Haines Hall on the beautiful, iconic UCLA campus - all curious about social media – what it is, what it does, and why anyone in business should care. The room was buzzing. It was exciting, to say the least. On top of that, the air conditioner broke during the morning, and as the buzz rose, so did the heat. But that didn't deter anyone. I thought for sure we'd lose people during the lunch break, but they all came back - in fact, they couldn't get enough.

From there, I developed the very first set of Social Media Marketing courses for UCLA Extension for launch in 2008. Classes were packed. We were turning people away. I decided to create a business conference, to be held on campus that would focus specifically on social media for the business community.

Gravity Summit[29], the new venture founded with the wonderful Rodney Rumford, was born, and we toured a number of campuses – UC Irvine, Stanford, Harvard, and then on to New York City.

Our event at the Harvard Faculty Club in 2009 featured MC Hammer and Gary Vaynerchuk (GaryVee and VeeFriends nowadays). It was also streamed by CNN.com LIVE. Check out the video above and remember, this was 2009, so streaming anything was brand spanking new. We were so far ahead of our time. Again.

It was in New York that McGraw Hill was in the audience sitting next to a former student of mine. We all got to talking afterward, and not too long after that, McGraw Hill asked us to write a book on Social Media Marketing. *The Power of Real-Time Social Media Marketing*, expertly co-written by Teri Thompson, was published in January 2011.

I continued the consulting and strategic advising business that was almost totally related to social media and new ways of communicating. Podcasting was not really a thing yet, mostly because people still thought podcasting required an iPod. By the way, that might have been great marketing on Apple's part, but it sure confused the business community.

The book we wrote was not intended to be a 'how to' on social media – others would write that book. It looked at the market strategically and tried to answer the question, WHY? Why is this happening now? What does it mean? We featured case studies from the American Red Cross, Mazda USA, DirectTV, and more. The book went on to be a best-seller in the category and to be used in many universities and still sits on corporate executive bookshelves.

In 2014, I received the following email:

Subject: Aston Martin

Ms. Macy,

My name is Michela Gilli, and I'm a sports marketing consultant working for some of the most known companies in the world, such as the NBA, Nike, and Aston Martin.

I was fortunate enough to find your book (The Power of Real-Time Social Media Marketing) at UCLA last year. The book is inspiring and driving me in my recent assignment in Aston Martin: the digital development of the company.

I'll be in Los Angeles from June 8th to the 12th, together with the Aston Martin Managing Director, and we would like to have the chance to meet you and discuss the role of social media in the luxury market.

We are hunters of excellence, and to me, you are paramount in social media.

Hope we will have the opportunity to get in touch with you.

To be perfectly honest, my first reaction to this email was that I did not believe that it was authentic. (Catfishing was not a well-known term yet). That is a reflection of the world we live in, don't you think? I responded, and I met Michela Gilli and Katia Bassi for lunch in June 2014. Katia was the Vice President of Aston Martin Lagonda and Managing Director of AM Brands at the time. I have been working with this group and the iconic brands Aston Martin and then Lamborghini from there to the present. And let me tell you, Motor Valley in Italy is absolutely one of the most exciting places on earth right now with the advent of electric vehicles in the luxury space. Reminds me of early Silicon Valley – beautiful location, very smart people, lots of positive energy and buzz.

The beautiful part of this story is that excellence finds excellence. Also, responding to inquiries with caution is not a bad thing. In spite of all the technology of today, people still do business with people, and building relationships still matters.

I have continued teaching at UCLA Extension and UCLA Anderson School of Management. I love being with students, and I love the environment of learning. Even to this day, I love hearing from a student a month or a year later as they embark on their professional and life journey. I am honored that they remembered me and were inspired by my class. It's an absolute joy to know that I have made a positive difference in someone's life, however small. I owe this to those who advised and helped me along the way, and I am a big believer in giving back.

- *"I wanted to thank you. You helped me in preparing for the job of my dreams, and I wanted to let you know that I got the position!"*
- *"…The things I learned in class made my promotion possible! I look forward to coming back to UCLA Ext and*

taking more classes with you! Hope you're well, and thank you for the confidence you instilled in class and personally 🖊 "

- *"Beverly is an amazing instructor! Throughout the class, she made sure everyone understood concepts correctly and answered all questions until everything got clear in our minds. She provided up-to-date information, gave insights about the industry, and challenged us to work on our own personal brand. Thanks to her, we had the chance to meet with some amazing guest speakers!*
- *"Outstanding instructor. Very knowledgeable and engaging. My best instructor so far! And I've taken over 10 courses so far at UCLA."*

And now here we are with NFTs and Web3. On August 30, 2022, I launched the first UCLAx course entitled, 'NFTs and Web3 for Business'[30]. This 90-minute webinar featured Keith Grossman, President of TIME Inc., and Kyle Schember, CEO of Subtractive, the company that launched the NFTs for charity with citizen astronaut Dr. Sian Proctor. We had over 400 registered participants for the webinar. Again, we made history.

We are standing on the doorstep of another significant time in the history of technology and massive change. A couple of people asked me in late 2021 if I was planning to write another book. "No way!" But I started thinking about it and thought that if I *WAS* going to write a book, it would chronicle my journey through these technology milestones up to the NFT and Web3 present.

I also decided this book, this literary effort, needed to incorporate the NFT experience in some way. This idea ultimately produced this experience which now includes the book *Imagine That... From PCs to NFTs*, as well as collaboration with other creators in art, music, and more.

The journey from PCs to NFTs seems long, but it is not, really, in the scheme of things. Forty or fifty years is just a blip on the radar when you think about it. And yet think of the massive changes we've seen since the technological breakthroughs of the 1980s.

Here we are at the start of 2023. The trend cycles continue, and I am thrilled to be here for quantum computing, AI, VR/AR, 3D printing, blockchain, cryptocurrencies, NFTs, genomics, robotics, space travel, and so much more. The world is rapidly evolving, and sometimes, it seems like too much. I am here to help make sense of it all, put it in context, and help provide a strategy for success in maximizing these new opportunities.

Chapter 3

Strategies for Success

Successful strategies for NFTs and Web3 technology involve a long-term approach to meeting the needs of the market and fulfilling business expectations. Most companies already have a digital transformation strategy in place, which provides a road map for successful digital transformation.

In addition to the focus on digital transformation and now NFTs and Web3, other trends are also emerging. These include the future of work initiatives, such as remote work and flexible hours, as well as new job opportunities and categories. There are also major advancements in funding for entrepreneurs and technology, including in the areas of DeFi, EdTech, AgTech, MedTech, SpaceTech, the metaverse, and more.

To succeed in this rapidly changing environment, it is important for businesses to stay up-to-date with these trends and adapt their strategies accordingly. By embracing NFTs and Web3 technology, companies can think about how to take advantage of new opportunities and create value for their customers and stakeholders. There is a lot to look forward to.

"The Trend is Your Friend"

This is a well-known saying in the investing world, and it sometimes applies to corporate development as well. Seizing the tailwinds created by trends in industry and technology can be pivotal to positive business results. Not reading or ignoring trends clearly can create setbacks and cause damage.

Trends matter to professionals, brands, businesses, and societies. Remaining relevant in this ever-changing world is critical, and understanding how thinking is changing and evolving or how people, in general, are viewing a certain subject or concept can help inform critical thinking. Smart brands will use this to their advantage.

It seems that NFTs arrived just in time, and we shouldn't be surprised at their success. Consumers have been demanding control of their data, subscription services are skyrocketing, and socially irresponsible firms have been struggling. Are these fads or trends? When do these 'fads' turn into 'trends'? And why does that matter?

What is the difference between a fad and a trend? Fads come and go and usually last a short time before gradually fade out. Over the years, there have been tons of fads that captured consumers' attention – remember Beanie Babies or Cabbage Patch Kids? What about fidget spinners or thick eyebrows? Or Crocs with socks?

Trends, on the other hand, are defined as "a general development or change in a situation or in the way that people are behaving." Trends can be an extremely reliable source of understanding which way the wind is blowing. Trends can give early warnings about what is correct and what might be a barrier to a brand's success. Tracking trends can help create a reliable system for discovering sources of change.

NFTs and Web3 are moving into "Trend" status. The market culture emerging around NFTs is one major indication that something meaningful and lasting is taking place. IP from the Bored Ape Yacht Club (BAYC) and CryptoPunks are by now legendary. Each of these communities rose up during the initial hype of NFTs and rapidly gained prominence in both earning power as well as potential IP rights for their holders and more.

Trend analysis can improve a business by helping to identify areas within the organization that are doing well as well as areas that are not doing well. In this way, it provides valuable evidence to help inform better decision-making around longer-term strategy as well as ways to futureproof the business.

That said, know that Web3 is on the move. Like it or not, AI, Web3, NFTs, tokens, blockchain, metaverses, AR/VR, and all the rest are here and not going anywhere. We are in 1994 of the Internet - before Google, eBay, Yahoo!, YouTube, iPhone, and the rest. New processes will be discovered, new thinking will be required, and it couldn't be more exciting.

Strategic Considerations

For those entering the NFT and Web3 space, the first and most important consideration is to engage in education around the technology and the culture of NFTs and Web3. Even though blockchain technology and cryptocurrency are a bit complicated, it is important to gain a basic understanding of how these technologies are similar and different from what is in use now in Web2. This book helps with that, and there are courses being designed as we speak.

It is also critical to gain an understanding of the new culture that is emerging around Web3 – that of the value of community and the concept of ownership and utility.

There are many misconceptions about NFTs, and education will help executives make informed decisions about when and how to get involved in this new space. As with any investment, it is important to become informed before jumping in. Companies that unlock the art of utilizing new technologies to attract and retain customers will be poised to generate sustainable, profitable growth and will end up winners.

The bottom line is that NFTs are here now. Yes, we are in a bear market cycle right now, but that is actually a good thing for the movement long term. Bear markets have a way of eliminating some of the worst 'riff raff' and spurring on the 'real work' in terms of development.

Even if you are not part of the NFT/Web3 culture right now, it's important to start preparing. The best place to start is with your brand – whether that's your personal brand or your company brand. I predict that even those who are not directly involved in Web3 off the bat will benefit from the "Own your own IP" concept that prevails in the new movement, no matter what. Therefore, understanding some of the drivers will be critical.

Current NFT and Web3 watchwords are *ownership, transparency, value, intellectual property, digital assets, utility,* and *community.* Consumers use these criteria to measure a brand's promise. If the brand's NFT project does not deliver, the company will definitely hear about it from the robust community.

The Web3 culture believes that for too long, we've been giving our valuable intellectual property away to platforms, companies, groups, and others, without any thought of compensation. The bad old days of Web2's 'do this for us and you'll get great exposure' are OVER. Settling for the 'exposure is your compensation' fallacy is so Web2!

Ask brands early in the NFT world who have tried that old Web2 line, and the evidence is clear. This next generation does not have it – whether deep into Web3 or not. Much like with Web1 and Web2, authentic presentation and experimentation will help achieve greater adoption. That includes a new understanding of ownership and compensation.

As the use cases in Chapter 4 will illustrate, thinking of NFTs as part of overall digital linkage to the consumer is part of the promise of NFTs. Learning buzzwords and trying too hard will not be authentic and will not work. Over time, brands must uncover what works for them and resonates with their consumers through trial and error and observing what succeeds and fails for others.

The ability to redefine the way brands engage with their consumers has included offering NFTs as digital art & collectibles, digital avatars, events and ticketing, and access/unlockable content. Brands ranging from fashion to professional sports to consumer goods are already experimenting with some of these NFT solutions in various ways.

Getting Started

To get started with NFTs and Web3, there are a few key steps that you can take. First, you will need to understand the basics of blockchain technology and how it powers the creation and use of NFTs. This can involve doing some research and reading up on the technology, as well as joining online forums and communities where you can learn from others who are already using NFTs and Web3.

Once you have a basic understanding of how NFTs and Web3 work, you can start exploring the different platforms and tools that are available for creating, buying, and selling NFTs. This can include blockchain platforms like Ethereum, as well as specialized NFT marketplaces and applications. You can also look for tutorials and guides that can help you get started with creating your own NFTs and can give you tips on how to manage and store your NFTs securely. Formal courses and classes are emerging on the scene as well.

As you begin to use NFTs and Web3, it can be helpful to start small and experiment with different applications and use cases. This can help you to gain practical experience with the technology and can give you a better understanding of the potential benefits and drawbacks of using NFTs and Web3 in different contexts. You can also join online communities and forums where you can learn from others who are using NFTs and Web3 and can share your own experiences and insights. By following these steps, you can get started with NFTs and Web3 and begin to explore the many exciting possibilities of this technology.

Be Practical

In the rapidly evolving world of NFTs and Web3, it is important for businesses to carefully consider their approach and find the strategy that works best for them. While some companies may choose to take a first-mover approach and launch their own NFT projects, others may prefer to adopt a fast-follower strategy and learn from the successes and challenges of early adopters. Latecomers may also be able to benefit from the experiences of others, avoiding common pitfalls and taking advantage of emerging best practices.

Ultimately, the key is to be practical and thoughtful in your approach. This may involve conducting market research, building internal expertise, and forming partnerships with industry leaders. By taking a measured and strategic approach, businesses can effectively navigate the rapidly changing landscape of NFTs and Web3 and position themselves for success in this exciting new era of digital innovation.

Brand Opportunities

As consumers become more comfortable with the Web3 environment, they are becoming more aware and concerned with how their favorite brands are getting involved. This offers an excellent opportunity for brands and organizations, particularly those with media and entertainment assets, to look to layering NFT strategy with 'traditional' consumer strategies and determine how best to gain a durable competitive advantage.

NFTs and Web3 provide brands with new opportunities for engagement that the big social platforms do not. Smart brands are looking at NFTs to engage directly with their fans and customers around custom content outside of the Web2 platforms to form connections with them that allow for real audience ownership and access.

Brands have spent years building up followers on Facebook and Instagram but are not able to communicate fully with those followers without paying the platforms to reach them. They are now wondering, "Why should we keep paying the 'middleman' for access when we did all the hard work in building the follower base?" NFTs change all that and give the reins back to the brands.

And yet it is so early in NFTs and Web3 that while the excitement and potential revenue opportunities are on the horizon, there is a certain amount of FUD (fear, uncertainty, and doubt) about the space. Even so, it is wise to start getting involved to be prepared and set up to benefit from a future that's coming fast.

Brands that are seriously considering how NFTs can benefit their business can consider these opportunities:

Know Your Value Proposition

Before jumping into the world of NFTs, it's important to take a step back and think about what value they can offer your brand. NFTs can be used to create unique digital experiences, such as exclusive content or virtual experiences, that can engage and delight your audience. They can also be used to create scarcity and exclusivity around your brand, which can increase its perceived value and desirability.

New Revenue Streams

Physical and digital commerce is entering a new phase. Some brands are minting NFTs as digital products with great success. Whether as collectibles or for use in a (future) Web3 environment, digital assets are beginning to gain ground with consumers. Thanks to the gaming industry, virtual goods and services are not a new concept. NFTs are also becoming available in digital formats that interface with augmented reality and virtual worlds.

NFTs can be linked to tangible items in the same manner that barcodes are used as identifiers. In the very near future, most fashion goods we purchase will be tokenized on a blockchain and uniquely identified. The NFT technology will guarantee the traceability, authenticity, and transparency of the transaction.

This will not only provide immutable provenance, but it will also help with the problem of return fraud which eats into a brand's profit margin.

Digital Customer Loyalty Programs

According to recent reports[31], the global loyalty market is valued at USD $7.8 billion, and NFT Tech is poised to use NFTs to drive the future of these programs.

To improve digital customer loyalty programs, one potential approach is to incorporate the use of NFTs in the rewards system. Because NFTs are unique digital assets that can be authenticated and verified on the blockchain, they are well-suited for personalized rewards, membership passes, and gated access to exclusive services and content.

Using NFTs in loyalty programs can offer a number of benefits. First, they can provide a more engaging and immersive experience for customers, as they can unlock personalized privileges and experiences that are tailored to their individual preferences and interests. Second, NFTs can be easily integrated into existing loyalty program platforms and systems, allowing companies to quickly and easily add new features and benefits to their programs. Third, NFTs can provide a level of security and authenticity that is not possible with traditional rewards systems, ensuring that customers are receiving the rewards they are entitled to and protecting the value of the rewards they earn.

To implement this approach, companies can work with third-party blockchain initiatives that have the technical expertise and infrastructure needed to develop and deploy NFT-based rewards systems. These partnerships can help companies gain access to the necessary technology and expertise while also allowing them to leverage the growing popularity of gaming dApps and the broader NFT ecosystem.

By combining the benefits of NFTs with the proven effectiveness of digital customer loyalty programs, companies can create rewards systems that are more engaging, personalized, and secure than ever before.

NFTs for Charity

Brands are using NFTs to promote a new type of fundraising in which those who donate funds are rewarded with a special NFT or collectible for their donation. This helps the brand generate awareness. It can also improve public perception and raise awareness for a cause.

Another potential strategy is to provide donors with more information and transparency about how their donations are being used. This could include providing detailed reports on the impact of the donations, as well as information about the specific programs and initiatives that the funds are being used to support. By providing this type of information, brands can help to build trust and credibility with donors and can demonstrate the value and effectiveness of their fundraising efforts.

In addition, brands can work to integrate NFT-based fundraising with other forms of philanthropy and social impact initiatives. For example, they could partner with organizations that are focused on specific causes or issues and could use NFTs to raise funds and awareness for these organizations and their work. This could help to create a more seamless and cohesive experience for donors and could help to drive greater impact and engagement across the philanthropic sector.

Building Community

In the early days of social media, many said that conversation was the new currency. The old marketing slogan, "Control the message", was out the window. Social platforms enabled consumers to 'talk back' to brands via blogs, comments, review sites, Twitter posts, and more. Quite frankly, it shocked brands. Not everything was complimentary or 'nice'. Some brands panicked. Consumers had something to say and weren't shy about speaking up.

Eventually, brands learned to 'listen', and social listening became a critical new skill. The concept of developing a 'conversation' between the brand and the consumer was born, and brands learned to be more nimble regardless of who was driving the conversation.

In Web3, the community is king. It is becoming clear that the NFT ecosystem is fundamentally different, and brand strategies will need to adapt. One of the most famous NFT communities to date is the Bored Ape Yacht Club. This community demonstrated in real-time what the rapid rise of enthusiasm and engagement could accomplish. Many believe it holds the key to their ultimate success.

New Approach to IP Rights

The Bored Ape Yacht Club (BAYC) is an NFT collection of 10,000 unique Bored Apes that are programmatically generated from over 170 traits, including expression, clothing, and headwear. Each BAYC NFT acts as a membership card that grants the holder access to exclusive benefits, such as additional NFT collectibles and access to the BAYC Discord server. The company behind BAYC, Yuga Labs, recently purchased the intellectual property (IP) rights to the iconic CryptoPunks and Meebits NFT collections. This means that BAYC and CryptoPunks owners now have the ability to use and exploit the IP rights to their characters commercially.

This is a significant development in the world of NFTs and IP rights. Previously, the rights to NFTs were typically restricted, limiting the ability of owners to use their NFTs for commercial purposes. However, the BAYC and CryptoPunks collections are now offering owners unrestricted rights to their NFTs[32], allowing them to create and sell derivative works based on their NFTs. This opens up new opportunities for NFT owners to profit from their collections and could help to drive further growth and innovation in the NFT space.

In Chapter 4, you'll read about Jenkins the Valet, an NFT owned by Tally Labs that has created an entire ecosystem around the Bored Ape they've named Jenkins the Valet. Jenkins the Valet even has his own CAA talent agent[33], highlighting the potential for NFTs to be used in new and exciting developments in this rapidly-evolving field. We are truly in a brave, new world. Imagine That!

Takeaways

- **Get Educated:** Even if your brand is not looking to enter into NFTs or Web3 anytime soon, you must become knowledgeable about what's coming. It would be business malpractice NOT to know what's around the corner. Get your senior team up to speed as soon as possible.
- **Best Practices:** Brands like Coca-Cola, Taco Bell, Tiffany, and many more are launching NFT and Web3 initiatives every day. Subscribe to 1 or 2 newsletters and appoint someone to become a subject matter expert to keep the senior teams informed. This is moving fast, and you want to keep up.
- **Be Strategic:** Allocate the appropriate time and energy to this new space. Find the balance between going down the blockchain rabbit hole and keeping your head in the sand.
- **Talent Acquisition:** Scan your internal environment for hidden gems, then find the best talent out there. It's a new world, and people are popping up in the talent pool with new skills and a whole new way of working. Don't be afraid of what's new.
- **Embrace Collaboration:** Most brands do not have the know-how or resources to go into this alone. Get used to the idea that you will want to collaborate with other brands and new NFT–genesis companies to get started.

Strategic Headwinds – Moving from Web2 into Web3

Many are anxious to embrace this brand-new paradigm and leave the old world behind. "That's SO Web2" is actually now a critical statement.

As the world continues to move from Web2 to Web3, it is important for individuals and brands to understand the strategic headwinds that are shaping this transition. While there are many exciting opportunities in the Web3 environment, it is also important to remain cautious and aware of the potential challenges and pitfalls that come with this new paradigm.

One key issue is the co-existence of Web2 and Web3 during this transition period. Many of the platforms and business processes that we rely on today are still rooted in the Web2 world, and it will take time for Web3 to become fully integrated into our daily lives. Web2 has billions of users and is not going away. Web2 and social platforms have enabled users to share opinions and information with others for years now, creating new ways of organizing and connecting with other people and have promised a greater degree of collaboration.

There are some good business practices in Web2 that won't be suddenly abandoned. This means that we are currently in a hybrid world where Web2 and Web3 co-exist, and this transition period is sometimes referred to as Web 2.5.

Another key challenge is the onboarding process for Web3. Understanding the financial implications of digital currency and the complexities of the NFT market can be difficult for those who are new to the space. In addition, the controversy over royalties and the legal ramifications of IP licensing and rights are just now starting to surface, making risk management and policy development more important than ever.

It is also important to remain somewhat cautious in the use of Web2 platforms and services. The expansion of social media has brought with it a number of challenges and drawbacks, including online stalking, cyberbullying, and the spread of disinformation and misinformation. As we continue to move into the Web3 world, it will be important for individuals and brands to understand how to protect their own intellectual property and data and to be aware of the potential risks and pitfalls of relying on Web2 platforms and services.

We could be in this transition for quite some time. It took almost ten years for email to become ubiquitous. Yes, things are moving fast, but even so, here we are two years into the space, and only a tiny fraction of the world knows about or cares about NFTs and Web3.

In Web2, your IP (intellectual property) is 'owned' and stored on the centralized platforms of BigTech via your personal data. By the way, we all gave that data voluntarily to Facebook, Twitter, Snapchat, Instagram, TikTok, etc. And we were very detailed – not just name and email or phone number, but we filled out every category - favorite music and entertainment, pastimes, travel destinations, health information, siblings and family members, political and religious affiliations, favorite books, sports teams… on and on.

Separately, this information seems pretty innocuous. But in the hands of the BigTech data masters and data wizards, this information has often been weaponized via advertising and social engineering to try to get people to do things or believe in things they might normally not believe at all. The irony is some even think these beliefs are their original idea.

All those pictures and funny videos that we uploaded are not ours, either. Just read the fine print on the Terms of Service for just about every BigTech platform. As they say, the platform is free to use, so YOU must be the product.

It's true that Web2 social media platforms enabled 'creators' to produce content, build a fan base, and then monetize that fan base relatively easily – sometimes in massive numbers. Then the platforms would profit from highly sophisticated personalized advertising while at the same time retaining ownership of all the content and data that could then be sold to advertisers. This endless circle, tightly controlled by algorithms, is enormously profitable – just not to YOU, the originator of the content and data.

As Web3 grows, it will fall to the individual to understand how to manage and protect their own Intellectual Property and their digital assets in a new way – not something most consumers have given a second thought to before. Now is the time to start paying attention. Your IP is valuable, even if you do not consider yourself a creative person. Why else would BigTech platforms spend so much time accumulating, selling, and manipulating your data?

Beware! Social Media is Tricky and Sticky

I co-wrote one of the first Social Media Marketing books with Teri Thompson in 2011, *The Power of Real-Time Social Media Marketing*. It was published by McGraw Hill. We didn't have an agent – the publisher heard my presentation on social media for business at a conference in New York City and asked us to write the book. It was a heady time – the promise of connectivity and collaboration with people around the world was exciting. It turns out we were a bit naïve.

Here we are, almost 12 years later... and WTF has happened to social media?!? The quest for the best in us seems to have degenerated into the worst in us.

Or has it? After careful analysis, I'll say... it depends. From a macro level, social media started out giving everyone a voice. That seems like a very good thing. Then it got really noisy. And loud. And those who screamed loudest got the attention. At the same time, many of the barriers to entry for creating content were torn down. I warned about 'metadata' in that book – and that is the giant pitfall we've all fallen into, like sheep running over the cliff.

Your Brand in Web3

With all of this in mind, let's remember that it's very early in this new cycle to be thinking about how you will present yourself and/or be perceived in Web3 because Web3 is not yet ubiquitous. But it will be.

As an aside, if you have kids between the ages of 7 and 13, most likely, they are on Roblox and/or Minecraft. These are metaverses. This demographic – GenA or GenAlpha is already adopting avatars and personas. They are buying and selling digital assets. They are growing up with this.

As adults, you will be faced with being reduced (or elevated) to an avatar sooner than you think. What will that mean? This is very much like the early days of social media when having just an EGG on your Twitter account was a big faux pas. Back then, individuals and brands started thinking about HOW they wanted to be represented. Should you be smiling, should you be in a group, should you be serious?

Should the photo be of the brand logo or the product? We had major conversations with clients about establishing their 'social voice' and how important it would be to represent that authentically. Web3 will be similar. Start thinking about that now.

Personal Brand Strategies for Success

As Web3 continues to grow and become more ubiquitous, it will be important for individuals and brands to think carefully about how they want to present themselves and be perceived in this new environment. In Web3, individuals and brands may be represented by avatars, which can have significant implications for how they are perceived and interacted with by others.

Having a well-defined personal brand helps build trust and credibility within the Web3 community and can make it easier for them to connect with others and build their network. A strong personal brand can also position individuals as authorities in their field and make it easier for them to be found by media outlets.

In addition, it will be important for individuals to develop a clear and consistent voice and tone in Web3, just as they would in any other online environment. This can help to establish credibility and trust with the Web3 community and can help to create a more engaging and immersive experience for users.

How do you want to appear in this new virtual world? If nothing else, being on Zoom for two years taught all of us that digital presence is strategically important. Lighting, posture, and body language – all come through in new and sometimes jarring ways.

How will you want to appear in a completely virtual world environment? As yourself? As an avatar? As a series of avatars, depending on your mood?

What will you (or your avatar) wear? How will you sound? What does your environment (office, home, outdoors) look like? These are all new areas to think about, and areas brands and businesses need to be thinking about.

A well-defined personal brand that clearly articulates who you are, what you do, and what value you bring to others makes it easier for other people and brands to see value in connecting with you. You can leverage your personal brand to build your network, both online and offline, quickly and effectively. Over time, your business will evolve. You may even start multiple businesses in different industries over the course of your career. Your personal brand stays with you as you move from one venture to the next.

As mentioned, going deep into the NFT and Web3 world presents a whole new set of challenges for all of us in determining who we want to be and how we want to be perceived in virtual worlds. More about that later, but this section will help you build a sturdy foundation in the digital space.

In addition to building trust within your community and your audience, your personal brand positions you individually as an authority in your field. Having a personal brand makes it easier for you to be found by media (online publications, magazines, television, radio, podcasts, etc.).

Getting Noticed

Not that long ago, the thinking was, "build it, and they will come". From Influencers to brand deals, to sponsorships, to TV deals for YouTubers, and even TikTok deals… the list goes on and on - put content out there, and voila! It goes viral. WOW. That was so easy, right? They love us! What's to worry?

Not exactly. The fact is that 'going viral' rarely happens organically. There is almost always paid media behind the viral 'hit'. Building it and no one coming (without a lot of help) is much more realistic. And even if they do come, are they real or bots/trolls? Are they buying? Are they transacting? Are they clicking through on the call to action? Are they engaging?

Even though business today can be super exciting, in the real world, doing business and getting business takes strategic planning, critical thinking, and persistence. It takes that fantastic vision you have AND the right actions to make it happen. Finding success is not easy. That doesn't mean it's so hard that you should just give up now, but it does mean that you want to approach this in a smart way so you can optimize your opportunities and engineer the best results possible. The same will be true in the virtual world as well.

It's challenging to get the 'right' job, navigate the startup world, find that work-life balance on a day-to-day basis without getting exhausted, and navigate interpersonal relationships with co-workers, colleagues, and customers. And in spite of the exciting developments, it is still a shark fest out there, and with all the changes going on, there are new pitfalls popping up. It's a lot to wrap your mind around and a lot to be aware of. Ghosting, horrible bosses, lack of training, outright lying or misleading on the part of the job seeker and the employer – it seems like everyone is looking for an angle.

Start now. Consider taking action in the form of a lookback or audit of your personal brand. Where do you stand currently? Then you can target where you want to go.

Your Brand in Transition

Your 'brand' matters, and building that brand and leveraging that brand is critical. What is your brand? What do people say about you when you leave the room? What motivates you? What are your strengths and opportunities? What is your value to others? There are many great exercises you can find online to build out your brand. I encourage you to do so. You need to know what you stand for and how you add value. And you need to be able to articulate that to others - verbally and via video first and then through work you do, conversations, projects, etc.

Your Digital Profile

Everything is digital in Web2 and will be virtual going into Web3. Most everything is mobile. Are your profiles up to date? Your photos? Any weird videos or posts you don't want others to see? Are your posts relevant to your brand? Are you lazy about your digital profile? A neglected profile tells the world that you don't care. You don't have to be a prolific poster – but you do need to think strategically. Your LinkedIn profile is now your business card. And no one will read your CV unless they need it for HR. The ABOUT section is The. Most. Important. Section. of the page and the first two sentences need to POP.

The Way We (You) Work

The WFH (work from home) concept born out of the last two years has literally changed everything. It's also put us on endless screen time with others in meetings and workgroups. That means the impressions we have of others and that they have of us happen virtually. What do people see when you enter into a Zoom meeting or interview? This is absolutely vital today.

How do you look? How's your posture? Are you slumping in a T-shirt, or are you facing front, dressed appropriately, and ready for business? What's in your background? How's the lighting? Can people hear you? Do you have good Zoom etiquette? Are you fidgeting and moving around, or are you still and attentive? Do you know how to mute and unmute? Are you prepared to share your screen or video if you need to? What are you wearing? Do you go off-screen? (A big NO, unless there is an emergency. It is disrespectful and shows disinterest.)

The Use Cases in Chapter 4 illustrate the transformative power of NFTs and Web3 when a commitment is made to learn and strategize, as suggested here. They also highlight creators and brands who are being thoughtful and strategic about their presence in Web3 and are positioning themselves for great success.

Chapter 4

Use Cases – Redefining Value

The use of case studies is a common and effective way to showcase the potential of NFTs and Web3 and to illustrate how businesses and organizations can benefit from these technologies. By presenting real-world examples of companies and organizations that have successfully implemented NFT projects, it is possible to provide clear answers to the common questions that people and businesses have about NFTs and Web3, such as how to assess the potential benefits, how to get started, and what to expect from the implementation process.

These case studies also provide valuable insights into the convergence of culture, technology, and commerce that is driving the growth of the new Ownership Economy. By examining the strategies, challenges, and opportunities that these organizations have faced, it is possible to gain a better understanding of the key trends and developments that are shaping the early stages of Web3.

Once people and businesses grasp the potential of NFTs and Web3, they start asking, "Would my business benefit from this? How can we best assess that? How do we get started?"

Those questions confronted the businesses and organizations featured in this chapter. The use cases I have gathered here are from top brands and rising companies who have launched NFT projects that illustrate best practices and provide clear answers to these questions.

They all found that education helped them navigate their road to success. Without exception, each knew that this was just the beginning and that these organizations would continue to evolve over time.

Doing the background work on these use cases, interviewing key people, and following the trail from beginning to end has been a transformative experience. I am pleased and delighted to introduce you to the dedicated groups of people quietly architecting major transformations and leading us into the new world of NFTs and Web3.

Time Inc. – TIMEPieces

NFTs in PUBLISHING

U.S. publisher TIME Inc. is blazing trails in a legacy business when it comes to NFTs. President Keith Grossman is focused on this new revenue stream with a goal to get there fast and then open it up to others.

The ability of a 99+-year-old legacy brand like TIME to not only re-invent itself via NFTs and Web3 but actually pave the way for others is absolutely brilliant. NFTs hit the radar of Keith Grossman, President of TIME Magazine in late 2020, and the rest is history.

Time continues to build on this success and expand its reach into other philanthropic areas – leading the way for others to follow in their footsteps.

Introduction

In September 2021, under Keith Grossman's strategic leadership and vision, the brand's Web3 community initiative called <u>TIMEPieces was launched</u>[34]. This project featured collaborations with leading NFT artists as well as artists who had contributed to TIME in the past. The *Genesis* drop and *Slices of TIME drop* have done more than $40 million in total sales volume. In many cases, this project and its revenue have been life-changing for contributing artists.

Taking this iconic media company into Web3 was no easy task. It took a deep dive into the space and education around blockchain, smart contracts and IPs, drop mechanics, NFTs, and more.

Keith gets huge props from his peers in the NFT space for embracing the concept of community building early on. This has been the key to this NFT project's success. Community building must be organic and authentic. In addition, it takes nurturing and attention to keep it fresh and growing. To Keith and the artists' credit, that community remains strong today and reinforces both the project and each other.

Use Case

Keith Grossman came to TIME from Bloomberg Media, where he was Global Chief Revenue Officer. Before that, he was at Wired (part of Condé Nast) and the news website Ars Technica. His forte is turnarounds and launches.

TIME is a respected brand with over 100 years of heritage, but it had been neglected for over ten years before the new owner Marc Benioff invested and allowed the team to experiment. Initially, the evolution was not to enter the crypto space; rather, the aim was to reinforce the core, modernizing TIME.com, the social channels, and the print magazine. This led to the launch of TIME Studios, the Emmy Award®-

winning film and TV studio which has produced many inspirational documentaries.

In March 2020, when Covid hit, and all his physical connections were taken from him, Keith came to the realization that his digital identity was just as valuable as his physical identity.

A self-confessed tech geek curious about the tech space, he started to look deeper and came across NFTs. He remembers, "…if my physical identity is just as valuable as my digital identity, here's a token that allows people to verify online ownership of something."

Keith pondered why he wouldn't want to own something online if he'd like to own it in the real world. He sat with the idea for a while until TIME owner Marc Benioff sent an email in February 2021 containing the sale results of the Nyan Cat NFT. It sold for almost $600k through the crypto art platform, Foundation.

The lightbulb moment followed when Keith connected the dots in his head and realized that for 99 years, what TIME had been doing was creating memes with its covers.

In the three years he'd spent at the publisher, every person he asked could tell him what their favorite TIME cover was, but if questioned about their favorite story, he didn't get the same response. In fact, only one person had an answer. Keith concluded that TIME is an inherently visual brand, not a written one, as everyone would assume.

And even though TIME Magazine is the brand's most familiar platform, it's also the smallest with 1.4m people, whereas the website has 25m, and the social channels garner over 70m.

In March 2021, Keith announced to Yahoo! Finance that TIME would be doing three things:

1. Selling 1-of-1 NFTs
2. Accepting cryptocurrencies for digital subscriptions within 30 days
3. Taking the next six months to learn the space and understand how TIME could use blockchain tokens to change the relationship with the brand

Not knowing all the answers, Keith just knew it was possible and that a tectonic shift from being online renters to online owners was coming, coupled with a tectonic shift of privacy moving from the platforms to the individuals.

He predicts a trend – a 20-year cycle where MoonPay essentially becomes the infrastructural organization of Web3, like Cisco for Web1 and Web2.

In September 2021, Keith and his team launched TIMEPieces, a Web3 community initiative from TIME that celebrates the work of artists - a core aspect of the TIME brand for nearly 100 years. It represents an important first step in TIME's Web3 community strategy, bringing together artists, collectors, and fans in a collaborative manner with the goal of building utility and community value over the long term.

Collectors could purchase TIMEPieces via a randomized, blind drop on nft.time.com. The drop consisted of a variety of editions totaling 4,676 pieces that were revealed once all of them were minted. Each TIMEPiece was priced at 0.1 ETH with the goal of attracting a wide array of collectors.

Owners of TIMEPieces can connect their digital wallets to the TIME site and receive unlimited access to TIME.com through TIME's 100th anniversary in 2023. They also receive exclusive invites to events and access to exclusive digital experiences.

The artists chosen to participate in the first collection reside in nearly every continent around the world and use a wide variety of approaches to their work ranging from photography to illustrations to paintings and more. Almost a quarter of them have produced covers for TIME in the past. Half have never created an NFT. Some of the pieces were still, and some were animated. All are completely original to TIME, and each piece in the collection was themed around the idea of "Building a Better Future."

TIMEPieces offers a significant benefit for its artists because the royalties shift the monetization from the moment of creation to the impact on society.

Following a stakeholder capitalism approach, all artists on primary and secondary sales split the royalties evenly with TIME in perpetuity, and the first 1% of TIMEPieces primary and secondary sales go to charity.

In its first year, over five collections, TIMEPieces featured 89 diverse artists of every discipline ranging from Nyla Hayes to music legend Timbaland. With 55,000 community members across Twitter and Discord and 20,000 NTFs, the initiative donated over $600k to charity while netting TIME around $10m of profit in the first year.

With everything the brand has achieved in the first year alone, what's next? TIME is focused on removing barriers to bring its Web2 individuals into its Web3 community.

With the trust that TIME has built over the past century, it can do things that other brands new to the space cannot, such as asking Deepak Chopra to speak to the community or helping Madonna enter the space. Access to events like this allows the community to decide who they want to self-identify with and which content they'd like to participate in.

Meanwhile, TIME Studios is actively working with communities such as the Robotos, the littles, and Toy Boogers to develop these communities into television shows, taking flat, static IP and creating new original IP.

With the knowledge TIME has amassed, it is helping other brands work out their approach and value proposition before they enter the space. One example is a four-way partnership with the city of Miami, Mastercard, and Salesforce to mint 5,000 NFTs on Ethereum. Designed by 56 local artists, the NFT sales drove revenue to local businesses while enabling new relationships between individuals and institutions.

It is clear that in Web3, traditional gatekeepers are no longer making the decisions; now, they are driven by the community.

Afrofuturism

NFTs and Art in OUTER SPACE

One of the most iconic figures in the world of outer space and now of Web3 and NFTs, Dr. Sian Proctor, was launched into earth's orbit as the pilot of the Inspiration4 all-civilian mission to space on September 15, 2021. As the pilot of this mission, Proctor became the first African American woman in history to pilot a spacecraft.

The significance of who she is, what she's doing in space, and her artistry combined with science and technology is unsurpassed. The importance of these milestones should not be lost on the Web3 community or the IRL community at large. It explodes with optimism, inspiration, mastery, and vision.

Dr. Proctor, who has a passion for space exploration and education, decided to create an NFT auction alongside the Inspiration4 mission to contribute toward the goal of raising two hundred million dollars for St. Jude Children's Research Hospital.

The NFTs were created using the Ethereum blockchain, which is a decentralized platform that allows for the creation and management of digital assets. The NFT is stored on the blockchain, which means that it is secure and cannot be altered or replicated.

Dr. Proctor partnered with Subtractive and Origin Protocol to conduct the three-day auction resulting in raising over four hundred thousand dollars for St.Jude. She also brought with her 101 NFTs from the Muttniks NFT collection. This collection represents the first canines that flew to space which paved the way for human space flight. The most famous of the dogs was Laika, who perished in orbit in 1957. As a reparational honor to the dogs who paved the way for human spaceflight, Laika in NFT form orbited the earth and returned safely.

Dr. Proctor's creative use of NFTs serves as a reminder of the incredible possibilities of space travel and the role that technology can play in making it a reality. As more and more people become interested in space exploration, NFTs like Dr. Proctor's could become an important part of the conversation, helping to inspire and educate people about the exciting possibilities of space travel and space settlement.

Overall, Dr. Sian Proctor's NFTs in space is a fascinating and innovative use of technology that showcases the potential of NFTs to revolutionize the way we think about ownership and value. As technology continues to evolve, it will be interesting to see how it will be used in the future and whether it will play a role in making space travel and space settlement a reality.

Use Case

Dr. Sian Proctor is a highly accomplished and multifaceted individual who has made significant contributions to the fields of geoscience education, exploration, space art, poetry, and astronautics. She is the first black female pilot to have flown an orbital spacecraft, and her work as an astronaut has helped to inspire and educate people around the world about the science that makes space travel possible.

Dr. Proctor has also played an important role in the development of the genesis NFT collection as part of the Going to Space project. This project features NFT art from a variety of artists, astronauts, engineers, and scientists, all of whom are dedicated to sharing their knowledge and passion for space with the wider community. "Seeker", which is part of this collection, is a limited-edition series with 100 NFTs. This piece introduces "adventure art" where the physical counterparts have journeyed to the Mariana Trench, The Titanic wreckage site, and onto outer space. The collection celebrates the science that makes space travel possible and what it means to explore and aims to inspire and engage the global space community through its vibrant and thought-provoking artwork.

Dr. Proctor's newest work focuses on Afrofuturism and has several useful applications. The Afrofuturism theme of her ongoing collections encourages conversations about the representation of women of color in the space industry as well as the Web3

community. She believes that when we solve for space, we also solve for issues on Earth and that we need to actively strive to create a just, equitable, diverse, and inclusive space (JEDI Space) both on Earth and beyond.

Dr. Proctor's NFT art collections are not only visually stunning and thought-provoking, but they also serve as a way for her to share her knowledge and passion for space with a wider audience. By bringing together the fields of art, science, and exploration, these NFT collections are helping to inspire and educate people around the world about the wonders of space and the amazing achievements that are possible when we push the boundaries of what we know and understand.

Dr. Proctor's work in space exploration has not only given her the opportunity to inspire and educate others about the wonders of space, but it has also allowed her to promote important causes and initiatives, such as sustainable food practices and the inclusion of women of color in the space industry. She's been a member of numerous boards and organizations, including the Explore Mars Board of Directors, the JustSpace Alliance Advisory Board, the Science in the Wild Advisory Board, the SEDS USA Advisory Board, and the National Science Teaching Association's Aerospace Advisory Board.

Dr. Proctor has spent many years as a professor, teaching geology, sustainability, and planetary science at South Mountain Community College in Phoenix, Arizona. She is currently serving as a member of the National Space Council Users' Advisory Group. She is also the CEO of Space2inspire and founder of The Proctor Foundation for Art and Science.

Throughout her career, Dr. Proctor has appeared on numerous international science shows and is currently featured on the Netflix documentary[35] "Countdown:

Inspiration4 Mission to Space". Her background and achievements make her a truly inspiring and influential figure in the fields of science, exploration, and space travel.

Jenkins the Valet – Tally Labs

NFTs in MEDIA

Jenkins the Valet is one of the first and most recognizable branded Bored Ape from the now-famous Bored Ape Yacht Club[36] *collection. The* Jenkins the Valet project[37] *is a groundbreaking example of the potential of NFTs in the creative industry, as it is a written word project at its core. This potentially paves the way for other authors and writers to create and monetize their work using NFTs. The project also places emphasis on the importance of community, as it allows members to join the Writer's Room via NFTs and participate in the creation of the narrative.*

In addition to being a unique and innovative concept, the Jenkins the Valet project also showcases the potential for NFTs to function as a multimedia experience. The book Bored & Dangerous by Neil Strauss, which is available to NFT holders digitally and physically, is just the beginning. The vision for the project includes incorporating gamified NFTs with an interactive experience that is unique to the Web3 environment.

Creative Artists Agency (CAA) is a leading entertainment and sports agency that has recognized the potential of NFTs to provide limitless opportunities for creators. CAA's Chief Metaverse Officer, Joanna Popper, believes that NFTs allow for a wide range of creative possibilities and has signed the owners of Bored Ape Yacht Club's Jenkins the Valet to work with them on opportunities across film, books, and podcasts.

Speaking at The Hollywood Reporter's Power Business Managers event in October 2022, Popper said: "Hollywood is always on the search for interesting new IP that has a built-in community, whether it's a book or platform or newspaper article that picked up a lot of buzz, there's a play here where you as the owner are able to then commercialize and do anything."

Overall, the Jenkins the Valet project is a pioneering example of the potential of NFTs in the creative industry and serves as a model for other creators looking to monetize and distribute their work in the digital world.

Use Case

It was the Bored Ape Yacht Club, owned by Yuga Labs, that broke the mold and introduced licensed commercial rights when it launched. What does this mean? It means that BAYC is creating intellectual property for the token holder. The rest is up to the owner.

In this case, an entrepreneur team (Safa, Valet Jones, and the rest of their company) is continuing to develop the IP around Jenkins the Valet, and the company, Tally Labs, oversees the business operations and infrastructural software development of Jenkins the Valet and all of their other IP.

In addition, this project not only monetizes and leverages their NFT asset but also includes an opportunity for others to join the Writer's Room via NFTs. This potentially blazes the trail for others. The vision for content creation and distribution – and most importantly, ownership – is unique to the NFT world and very inspiring.

The founders are adamant that they are writers first and foremost. It shows in what they are doing. The Bored Ape Yacht Club is one of the most iconic collections in the NFT space to date. The founders of Jenkins bought their Ape, named it Jenkins, and the rest is history.

Let's hear from them:

For a while, content has been created by a small group of executives in Hollywood and then distributed to the masses for a hefty price tag. We believe that amazing content can be created when individuals with all different perspectives from all over the world come together to harness their collective brainpower. Furthermore, we think the ownership model of the content should reflect that. We view what we're doing as the next evolution of how content is created, consumed, and owned.

The project Tally Labs has become most well-known for is what they are building with *Jenkins The Valet: The Writer's Room.*

First and foremost, Jenkins the Valet is an NFT character (Tally Labs) created who was inspired by Bored Ape #1798 (an asset we own). Jenkins is the first and one of the most well-known characters to emerge from the NFT space. We grew his following to 50,000 across Twitter and Discord by organically posting "in character" and writing stories about other Apes he came across.

Now, Jenkins has launched The Writer's Room, a tool for community-generative content, character building, and licensing. Holders of Writer's Room NFTs can access this gated platform and vote on the content that Jenkins and Tally Labs produce.

Over time, the Writer's Room software will expand our support stories from other characters and creators in the future. Our first project is a novel set in the Bored Ape Yacht Club and is written in partnership with 10x New York Times Bestseller - Neil Strauss.

Holders of our NFTs voted on the story arc that informed Neil's writing. In addition, the characters (4,075 of them!!) were licensed to us by thousands of individual Bored Ape and Mutant Ape owners.

We were able to facilitate this kind of mass licensing because each individual NFT holder owns the commercial rights to their own NFTs.

Our Objective

We believe that the next generation of household characters and worlds will originate on the blockchain. We hope to unlock this creativity by giving anyone with an NFT and an Internet connection the ability to bring these stories to life.

We create bottoms-up, NFT-native content with our community. We believe that building a strong community and bringing them along from day one creates a much stronger bond with the IP we collectively develop. Our strategy is to engage our community in all the content and IP that we create because we (1) think it will make for better work and (2) believe it will create a more organic connection.

We bring in mainstream, commercially successful artists (writers, directors, musicians) and pair them with an enthusiastic Web3 community ready to contribute. The two groups are intermediated by an intuitive software platform that is designed to distill creative direction and source robust character profiles. We believe that activating Web2 talent in an inherently Web3 way creates something special.

We've just closed on a $12m seed round led by a16z Crypto to continue building tools and creating IP at scale.

We believe that Web3 is putting the Internet back into the hands of individuals. It will look a lot like groups of individuals organizing freely around ideas and bringing those ideas to life in a way that brings value to the collective. We are excited to build things that enable this behavior.

We feel that after a Web3 community member has experienced the type of active engagement with content that we're offering (and believe will be standard), it's hard to go back. Imagine if, as a kid, you were able to help build Star Wars! Or Harry Potter, or Lord of the Rings! We believe the next generation of household IP will bubble up from these NFT communities.

'All Time High'

NFTs in MUSIC

Spottie WiFi, the creator of "All Time High'[38], is a pioneering figure in the NFT music industry, and his work is helping to pave the way for the wider adoption of NFTs in the creative sector.

Spottie WiFi, also known as Miguel Mora, is a leading figure in the NFT music industry. He received the 2021 NFTNYC award for Best Use of NFTs in the Music Industry in recognition of his hard work and deep understanding of the NFT and Web3 space.

Spottie is best known for his project that sold out in under 60 seconds and netted him over $192,000, but he also values his role as a guardian of the NFT space and is dedicated to sharing his knowledge and experience with others. He has worked with some of the biggest names in the music business, and his deep understanding of the technology and its potential has made him a respected authority in the field.

He has worked with some of the biggest names in the music industry, and his deep understanding of the technology and its potential has made him a respected authority in the field. Spottie believes that NFTs have the potential to revolutionize by enabling artists to connect directly with their fans and create unique, valuable experiences. He also believes that NFTs can expose the unnecessary role of middlemen in the industry and allow artists to develop a more sustainable business mode.

Introduction

Spottie WiFi's story is deeply rooted in NFT legend. He is now an icon. Miguel Mora created Spottie's persona after purchasing Punk 5528 on February 23, 2021. Spottie deliberately set out to pave the way for the NFT music revolution. It started with collaborating with hip-hop stars, including Bun B, and has continued with performances and recordings.

His investment into CryptoPunk 5528 positioned him as an icon in the music space. This was a strategic move by Spottie. The punk had spots on its face (a valuable rarity feature in the NFT world), and Miguel used this feature to create his avatar and alter ego Spottie WiFi. Key purchases into other major NFT communities like the Bored Ape Yacht Club and the Gutter Cat Gang increased his profile and footprint in NFTs and Web3 and brought credibility and inclusion into what is fast becoming the legendary NFT OGs.

Use Case

Working with producer Stefan Clark, Spottie released a seven-song album. He used his deep understanding of the importance of drop mechanics to create the following: The drop was limited to 2,000 copies. Each EP purchase came with a mystery mint NFT.

The purchaser also instantly obtained sync rights to the NFT's master recording, allowing them to use their song in a commercial, film, or television show and keep the profits. Each NFT holder can also receive a vinyl copy of the album. This is the project that sold out in under 60 seconds and netted him over $192,000.

The business and Web3 technology information Spottie shares is important. His 'alpha' has increased his stature in the space, and many turn to him now as a 'subject matter expert' regarding NFT drop mechanics and contracts.

Spottie believes NFTs are going to expose how unnecessary middlemen are. It also shows that artists don't need a million fans that might spend one dollar on them per year. With NFTs, an artist just needs 500 or 1,000 fans that really rock with them, want to see them succeed, and are willing to invest in their success.

From there, that artist might go on to develop a larger platform and following, then those early believers will be rewarded because NFTs offer them the potential for a return on that initial investment in a way that streaming or even buying MP3s does not. NFTs also offer the potential for artists to deliver much more utility than an MP3, like offering a copyright license and commercial usage rights or potentially even splitting royalties with fans.

Spottie says he is just getting started. His deep understanding of contracts, IP, drop mechanics and more continues to set the pace for others to follow. From his website:

Spottie's new album will include five NFT singles. "All Time High" featuring Bun B is Single #1, and "Full Set" featuring Gold-Rilla and Illa Da Producer is Single #2 (NFT coming soon). "I'm Spottie" genesis NFT holders will receive one free claim per wallet of the forthcoming NFT single drops via a snapshot that will take place prior to each release.

Anyone who collects one NFT from each of the five NFT single collections will be able to claim a free vinyl record of Spottie's new album, or they will be able to burn the complete set of five NFTs to claim a special album NFT that will provide additional utility.

Clube Atlético Mineiro

NFTs in SPORTS

Atlético Mineiro is the oldest active football club in Minas Gerais, Brazil, founded in 1908. This use case presents the benefits of NFTs: 1) as an investment, 2) as collectibles, 3) in ticketing, and 4) as a fan experience. Understanding that fans are passionate and hungry for as many of their favorite teams and their star athletes as possible is key.

NFTs and Web3 expand on that fan experience and offer a new way to engage and communicate and increase revenues. The ability to maximize the in-place community is key to their success. Currently, Felipe is the Director of Brazil, Socios.com

Sports and NFTs

The NBA's Top Shot was one of the first projects to take the plunge and create an NFT storefront. Top Shot is an NFT marketplace where fans can buy, sell and trade NBA moments, which are packaged highlight clips that operate like trading cards.

They specialize in what they call "Moments" on a Moment Marketplace. The MLB and NHL have followed suit.

This makes sense because it turns out that anything with a passionate fandom and associated collectibles is one of the most explosive areas of the NFT space.

Use Case

At Atlético, Felipe was exploring new ways of interacting with fans using blockchain, augmented reality, cryptocurrency, and NFTs. The group auctioned a digital piece of art as an NFT in May 2021 on OpenSea[39] and generated $40,000 in gross revenue.

Digital collectibles are cool, but to Felipe, the future of NFTs is unlocking experiences. And when he thinks about it, it's pretty clear that the ticketing business is going to be disrupted by blockchain.

"We started to study the possibility of selling tickets as NFTs because we could take advantage of all the features that the technology provides: first, fans can verify the authenticity of tickets; second, we can track who has the ticket and therefore who is coming to the stadium, because a lot of times the person that buys it is not the person that is going to use it. And last but not least, smart contracts allowed us to control the secondary market, generating a new revenue stream.

We used AI to find the perfect pricing for every sector on every match, based on information like the day of the week, match starting time, weather, the moment of the team, who we are playing against, if we have other events in the city at the same time or close, if it's a holiday's eve, if the match is at the beginning of the month or at the end because people will have more or less money to spend… So we had a lot of variables that we could use in order to have better pricing, and we wanted to start exploring it in the next season. Football clubs are media companies today, and there are so many types of content that we can explore.

We were not just a football club but a media company, and we wanted to provide the best content possible on our platform. The OTT was key for our strategy to reach fans worldwide, to generate a new revenue stream, but more than that, it's a first-party platform, so we owned the data, which was very important to us. This way, we could study fans' behaviors, what type of content they preferred to consume, how and when they preferred to consume it, and with which type of device.

At the time, we didn't own the rights to broadcast live matches of the professional Men's team, but we planned to show live matches of the Youth Academy and the Women's team and special content, like documentaries, total access series, All or Nothing style, and match analysis.

More than that, we explored other content formats that are not usual to sports organizations, like reality shows, game shows, podcasts, gastronomy, and travel programs, where the chef and the host are Atlético fans, kids' content… And even content that is not related to Atlético. Why not have the rights to show a league from a country that has not been broadcasted in Brazil, for example? I think that an OTT platform can "speak" to different kinds of audiences, and that's what we explored."

VanEck Asset Management

NFTs in FINANCIAL SERVICES

VanEck Assessment Management, an investment firm with over $82 billion in assets under management, has entered the metaverse by releasing a collection of 1,000 non-fungible tokens (NFTs) in May 2022. The move represents a significant investment in the potential of NFTs by a major financial institution.

The VanEck Community NFT is intended to cultivate engagement and community among those with a passion for finance and crypto. The NFT offers exclusive access to an inclusive community, providing early access to research, investment opportunities, and educational content. It also serves as a digital membership card, providing a sense of ownership and recognition within the community.

The launch of the <u>VanEck Community NFT</u>[40] *is a significant development in the adoption of NFTs by mainstream institutions. It signals the growing recognition of the potential of NFTs to provide value and utility to their owners and the communities they belong to.*

Introduction

Matthew Bartlett is the visionary behind the launch. His background clearly paved the way for this historic project. In his own words: "I first encountered an instance of the metaverse back in 2017. Decentraland, a virtual platform where you can buy and sell land, estates, avatars, and more, was just getting started. They created a world called Genesis City with a finite number of just over 90,000 parcels of digital land. On each parcel, you could theoretically build anything you wanted: a meeting place, a concert venue, or even a digital winery (I tried this and failed). It offered truly limitless opportunities. Its map was complete with roads, highways, *and* mini-communities just ready to be built until crypto winter took hold."

Use Case

Lasting from late 2017 until 2018, the crypto winter was a prolonged period of bearishness when asset prices fell over several months. It stifled the bullish mindset of some crypto enthusiasts and caused projects like Decentraland to experience a relative slowdown in content creation and interest in the project as a whole.

This slowdown seemed to last until early 2021. I invested mostly in coins and tokens throughout this period. Then a project tied to non-fungible intelligence—the ability to train your own AI in the form of an NFT or non-fungible token—pulled me back into a fascination with NFTs once more. This project reignited my passion for the space, and it was the perfect time to get re-engaged, as my employer, VanEck, was contemplating the idea of using NFTs for the purpose of building a community. They brought me on as a Special Advisor to the project, and I worked on the project with my other Co-Founders, JP Lee and Donna Pearson.

Use Case VanEck and Our Community NFT

VanEck is a U.S.-based, global asset manager that provides forward-looking, intelligently designed solutions, offering value-added exposures to emerging industries, including crypto and other asset classes. We recognized the need for education early on around digital assets and their potential use cases and have curated educational content covering all parts of the digital assets space.

In May 2022, we further embraced this role as a leader in blockchain-related investments with the launch of the VanEck Community NFT, the first-ever NFT offered by a global asset manager. 1,000 NFTs were created, and we received over 50,000 sign-ups on our NFT Community webpage.

As a fairly new technology, NFTs have become a coveted digital asset for projects, companies, and groups to distribute across various blockchains as a reward for investors, loyal followers, and community members. New participants to the space like to use art as an example to define what NFTs are. Art is a good use case, but not the only one. NFTs have been used to tokenize just about anything, from play-to-earn assets (video games where you earn actual crypto) to real estate, collectibles, and so on. NFTs are now providing real-world utility to their owners and broader communities.

One of the core tenets of the VanEck Community NFT was grounded in the need to cultivate engagement and community among those who have a passion for finance and crypto alike. Our objective was to bring folks together from different backgrounds and experiences in the hopes of fostering further educational opportunities, including the ability to network and collaborate as a community. Therefore, a digital membership card is the best way to describe the VanEck Community NFT. It offers exclusive access to an inclusive community that is both free and provides real-world utility. The NFT is distributed to holders who wish to have early access to research, be in the know for specific investment opportunities, and take part in real and virtual events and experiences sponsored by VanEck.

The beginning of our NFT idea started back in November 2021 and took about six months of development before it launched. We started with the idea of building a storyline around former Treasury Secretary Alexander Hamilton. This founding father was chosen as the initial face of the avatar, who we called "Hammy"—a futuristic version of Hamilton, who, as part of our storyline, believes that Bitcoin or decentralized networks and payments may positively disrupt financial markets. This was based on Hamilton's early "Report on the Public Credit", which was a defining piece that analyzed the financial standing of the U.S. and offered recommendations for reorganizing our national debt and establishing public credit. This was a very innovative idea and paved the way for the financial system we know today.

To support this storyline, the pre-reveal image of our NFT is tied to the popular meme, "Money Printer Go Brrr". The VanEck 3D avatars released at the end of May are ultra, high-quality avatars built on Unreal Engine 5, which in our view, are among the most advanced technologies to leverage when building interoperable assets. The avatars move and are supported with backgrounds and sounds, and more importantly, include a new set of diverse characters who will aid Hammy in his missions.

There is also a cast of historical "one of one" avatars. These famous scientists, inventors, and mathematicians helped to shape our current world and, coincidently, are also used as the names of VanEck's conference rooms at our home office. These famous contributors will be honored as the rarest and most legendary characters of the project. Additionally, the expanded utility will come with owning one of these tokens.

For supporting ongoing community engagement, we will be utilizing POAPs (Proof of Attendance Protocol) as a strategy for supporting and incentivizing an engaged community. POAPs are similar to digital badges that show proof on the chain that a user participated in a real-life or virtual event. As a project, we can then reward users who own multiple POAPs with future airdrops or additional experiences. This strategy will likely be adopted by other corporations who wish to onboard and interact with loyal brand supporters in the near future!

Moving forward with our roadmap, we will look to engage our community members with invites to various global events and even more. We're also excited to get their opinion and suggestions on where the community will go in the future.

Bottom-line, everyone in the VanEck NFT Community will have a voice, and we look forward to seeing what we can accomplish with our community as a whole.

Three Squares Inc. - PledgeCrypto

NFTs in ENVIRONMENTAL SERVICES

Although the NFT space is exciting and full of possibilities, the revelation that NFT production consumes enormous amounts of energy has raised red flags — and a search for sustainable solutions. Here's what you need to know. Jaime Nack has an impeccable reputation in environmental sustainability and works with corporations, governments, and real-estate developments around the world.

The proof of work (PoW) model, which is used by Bitcoin and other cryptocurrencies, consumes large amounts of energy and generates electronic waste. In contrast, the proof of stake (PoS) model, which is used by some cryptocurrencies such as Solana and Ethereum, is more energy-efficient and has a lower environmental footprint.

PledgeCrypto, a platform that allows donors to make cryptocurrency donations to non-profits, commissioned an environmental impact assessment by Nack's firm to quantify the carbon emissions of cryptocurrency transactions on its platform. The assessment found that using the PoS model instead of the PoW model could reduce the carbon emissions of cryptocurrency transactions by 99.95%. These findings highlight the increasing demand for sustainable solutions in the cryptocurrency and NFT space.

Introduction

The benefits generated via the NFT marketplace and the prevalence of cryptocurrencies throughout the globe are numerous and constantly expanding. Crypto promotes financial inclusion by driving innovation in financial services, and NFTs help artists expand their offerings, generate new and ongoing income streams, and unlock the world of 'collecting art' for those without yacht-sized budgets. However, to fully account for these benefits, it is important to understand the environmental impact of such activities.

The Process

Crypto relies on distributed systems that store and transfer ownership securely through a process based on complex computations on the blockchain. <u>The process matters</u>. Bitcoin utilizes the proof of work methodology (PoW), which involves miners competing to add a set of proposed transactions as a new block to the network by solving a mathematical challenge whose complexity adjusts with respect to available computational power. While there may be hundreds of thousands of computers racing to solve the same problem, only one can ultimately receive the Bitcoin honorarium. The mining activity required for the PoW model consumes large amounts of energy and has earned Bitcoin the status of holding the highest environmental footprint of all Crypto. Bitcoin consumes more electricity in a year[41] than the entire country of Argentina - around 110 terawatt-hours, according to the Cambridge Center for Alternative Finance (CCAF). Cryptocurrencies that rely on PoW validation also generate a large amount of electronic waste, as the miners tend to utilize a large volume of hardware for their operations.

In comparison with the PoW model, the proof of stake (PoS) model relies on participants, or "validators," to lock up set amounts of cryptocurrency or crypto tokens (their "stake") in a smart contract on the blockchain. In exchange, they receive a chance to validate new transactions and earn a reward. Solana, Terra, and Cardano are among the largest cryptocurrencies that use proof of stake. Solana, though it has suffered numerous outages over the past year, has proven itself in the NFT arena as it recently surpassed $1 billion[42] in all-time market volume at the beginning of 2022. DappRadar counts Magic Eden (an NFT marketplace on Solana) as the tenth most popular Dapp, ranked by a number of users.

By removing the competitive computing element, PoS systems reduce the energy required for mining and focus each machine on solving *one challenge* at a time. Environmental groups and impact investors alike praise the PoS model for its efficiencies and lower footprint. This type of external support for PoS drove Ethereum[43], the second largest Crypto by market cap after Bitcoin, to convert from PoW to PoS as part of its evolution to Ethereum 2.0. This process conversion will dramatically reduce the energy consumption of Ethereum-based tokens and blockchains by <u>an estimated 99.95%.</u>[44]

Use Case | PledgeCrypto

Pledge, the innovative fundraising service that simplifies donations for nonprofits through its online platform, designed <u>PledgeCrypto</u>[45] to allow donors to make Crypto donations. Prior to the launch of this new platform, Pledge realized the mining process used significant energy and contributed to global carbon emissions. As a result, PledgeCrypto commissioned the environmental consulting firm <u>Three Squares Inc.</u>[46] to conduct a cryptocurrency environmental impact assessment and quantify the carbon emissions of cryptocurrency transactions made on the PledgeCrypto platform.

"At Pledge, we fundamentally believe that unlocking Crypto donations will provide an abundant new source of funding for nonprofits around the globe, but the process needs to be done in a sustainable way," said James Citron, CEO of Pledge. "Inspired by our core values of care and community, we wanted to respond to environmental concerns about Crypto, which is why we are proud to lead with the first-of-its-kind patent-pending invention to ensure that every Crypto transaction through Pledge will support UN-verified projects. PledgeCrypto will not only be the most accessible way for donors to donate their digital assets and for nonprofits to receive them, but also the most environmentally conscious way in the industry."

Pledge easily tracks every cryptocurrency donation

transaction, accounting for how Bitcoin has the highest emissions per transaction and will retire carbon credits on an annual basis determined by total transactions and the environmental impact of the cryptocurrencies used.

Eight of the most used cryptocurrencies were evaluated to quantify the emissions associated with a single transaction. This in-depth analysis included the total estimated energy of the cryptocurrency, matched with published recent transaction volumes. A weighted electricity emissions factor was derived from the regional breakdown of transaction locations around the globe. Multiple data sets were also used to ensure optimal data integrity. While the final emissions vary based on the energy used, location, and the currency being donated, Pledge estimates that roughly <u>every 100 donations will generate approximately 2.6 tons of carbon dioxide (CO2) emissions</u>[47]. To compensate for this environmental impact, Pledge will offset 100% of the carbon footprint of each donation transaction at no additional cost to donors or nonprofits. Carbon offset projects, sourced from the <u>United Nations Climate Neutral Now Initiative</u>[48], will support the Burgos Wind Project and cooking stoves in Malawi.

Future Outlook

As the Crypto industry is only in its infancy and is constantly evolving, by the time of this book's release, there will be new solutions, new key players, and significant efficiency updates to existing platforms. These advancements will be accelerated due to shifting consumer expectations as well as international regulatory requirements. Regulations such as the EU Taxonomy and proposed SEC climate risk ruling in the U.S. will continue to push major corporations to track, measure, and lower their carbon footprints, and this movement will reverberate across the various digital systems.

Subtractive / St. Jude Children's Hospital

NFTs for GOOD

Combining NFTs and outer space is literally out of this world. The collaboration between Subtractive and Dr. Sian Proctor on the "Seeker" NFT project is a truly innovative and groundbreaking achievement that showcases the potential for combining NFT technology with outer space. The launch of the "Seeker" NFT on the Inspiration Flight not only marked a first in the world of NFTs, but it also helped to raise money for a worthy cause - St. Jude Children's Hospital.[49]

Dr. Proctor's impressive background as a geoscientist, explorer, space artist, poet, and astronaut adds an extra level of credibility and expertise to the project, and her participation helps to highlight the intersection of art, science, and education. The successful launch of the "Seeker" NFT and the successful fundraising efforts demonstrate how technology can be used to break down barriers and make a positive impact on the world. This use case is a testament to the potential of NFTs and the exciting possibilities that they offer in the realm of outer space and beyond.

Use Case

Kyle Schember is a well-respected producer and creative professional with over 25 years of experience in the industry. He is a co-founder of Subtractive, a Los Angeles-based collective that creates content for a variety of media platforms, including theatrical, broadcast, web, video games, retail, and live events. In July 2021, to mark the 70th anniversary of the first canine space travelers, Kyle and the team at Subtractive launched the Muttniks Genesis Collection by Cosmic Paws NFTs. This collection celebrates the famous Muttnik Laika, the first living being to orbit the earth in a spacecraft, and is a tribute to all of the amazing animals who have contributed to space exploration over the years.

A Lightbulb Moment

Today, Kyle and the creatives at Subtractive align with like-minded artists, filmmakers, storytellers, and dreamers. Focusing on expanding an emerging culture where music, art, and technology converge, the company nurtures and supports new hybrid forms of artistic expression and provides a platform to be seen, heard, and experienced.

Everyone who works at Subtractive is an incredibly talented artist or musician, and they share the same common passion for being creative. Operating out of an airplane hangar at Santa Monica, CA airport since the organization was founded, the area has evolved. Silicon Beach, as it is now known, is home to more than 500 technology companies.

In 2012, a friend of Kyle's flew down from San Francisco, opened his laptop in the Subtractive lobby, and said: "You need to know about this. This is you. This is how you think. It embodies all of what I think you'll love." Kyle was dubious, but when his friend broke it down, a lightbulb turned on, and he got a clear indication of the potential of blockchain.

He started talking about it enthusiastically, even when friends and colleagues were not open to listening, and some even thought he'd lost his mind. With the lack of interest from most people he spoke to, Kyle questioned himself, but he had ideas for auctions and preconceptions of what NFTs are and wrote several pitches. The connection point about where you could take a digital asset and have it immutable and tradable was very clear to him, and it was this that opened things up in his mind, but at that time, it was way too early for most people to get on board.

Later in 2012, Kyle attended the first Bitcoin conference in Las Vegas and took his accountant along. Although skeptical, they both got a great education from the people in the room, many of whom are still in the space today. This education and realization of what was possible cemented his desire to be involved in the market.

Covid & Clubhouse

Fast forward to 2020 and the Covid pandemic. With people stuck at home, many were on Clubhouse, where a community started to bubble up through this exciting new app that was just voices, allowing you to sit back and not be on camera. It offered a visceral experience, where you listen and feel what everybody else is experiencing. In Clubhouse rooms, one by one, each person would introduce themselves to the community. This fascinated Kyle as he could connect with all types of artists he'd never have known about pre-Covid. Emotionally moved by the experience, he realized that there were people all over the world looking for an outlet like this and a way to express themselves creatively and, importantly, be compensated accordingly for their work.

Kyle is a lifelong art fan and collector who has always visited art shows and galleries and attended concerts, but he hadn't really looked at other artists around the world. At this moment, he saw the bigger picture and realized something important was happening. And it was happening at a community level.

He observed the activity in the NFT market. There were 1-of-1s, fine art, and another movement of profile pictures (PFP) that represent people on their social channels, in other words, what a person connects to in generative arts. It was this medium that the team at Subtractive decided they should try their hand at first.

Muttniks

As a group, Subtractive is incredibly passionate about space, art, and music. A friend of Kyle's had given him a Russian poster of Laika, which had been on his wall forever. He kept walking by the poster and thought that this story of the first dog to fly to space would make an interesting collection.

Kyle assembled a team to experiment with no expectation of outcome. The result is the genesis collection 'Muttniks' by Cosmic Paws.

Muttniks is a series of illustrations all designed in-house. The colorful cartoons were fun, which made them well-received by the community. They also introduced a reveal, or NFT drop, so buyers bought a token and only saw what they had bought into on the reveal day.

Prior to Muttniks, Kyle had bought several NFTs in this way and had usually been disappointed with whatever he ended up with as he didn't have a connection to it once it was revealed.

So Subtractive invented a generator that would allow people to choose what they wanted instead of being allocated something randomly. This democratized the rarity.

Rarity comes into play with NFT collections as it's impossible to know ahead of time what the most valuable or rare one will be because it's a collective consciousness of every person who minted whatever they chose. If they decide not to mint it, that NFT goes into the trash, and they see something else. So, until the whole process is finished, there's no way to know which is the most interesting.

At that time, the concept was quite heavy, and many people didn't understand or care. This was a big lesson for Kyle. In the end, they sold 1,069 Muttniks NFTs, which they considered a success. Based on this success, they decided to continue with additional characters.

Muttniks has not enjoyed the fortune of Bored Apes, but the aim was to understand the process and build a community. Many lessons were learned from the experience; they connected with people who love space and dogs and built a community that is still alive today. At some point, they realized they were also building a brand. The project dropped on July 21, 2021. There were only a handful of NFT projects up to that point. Soon after, thousands of new projects launched every day, making it difficult not to get swept up in the hype and the noise.

NFTs for Good

On September 15, 2021, a privately chartered space flight dubbed 'Inspiration4' became the first crewed orbital mission with no professional astronauts on board. The crew consisted of four civilians.

The team at TIME Studios created a five-part docuseries for Netflix titled Countdown: Inspiration4 Mission to Space that chronicles the three-day SpaceX Dragon mission.

Part of the mission's goal was to raise $200m for the St. Jude Children's Research Hospital. The team at Subtractive saw an opportunity to get involved and create NFTs to be auctioned during the mission to benefit St. Jude's. They collaborated with 50 artists, including Nyla Hayes, Ryan Stuit, Nicole Stott, and Dr. Sian Proctor, an artist, and poet who was one of the Inspiration4 pilots.

Everyone worked on the project for free, with 100% of the proceeds going straight to help St. Jude Children's Research Hospital reach its goal. The auction went live the moment the rocket lifted off and ended when the crew splashed down. In three days, they raised over $400,000, which exceeded all expectations.

This was a second lightbulb moment for Kyle. The project and its outcome were important because everyone who was initially cynical or thought NFTs were stupid or the project was dumb had to sit up and take notice of this case study. No one took a dollar for their time, and it raised much-needed funds for the hospital. St. Jude's raised the full $200m target through collective efforts, and Kyle, the team at Subtractive, and all the artists involved were delighted to be a part of that effort while demonstrating what's possible in the NFT space.

It wouldn't have happened without the support of the team at Origin Protocol, who were key partners. Kyle met them at the LA Art Show and said: "You don't know me, but I'm going to ask you to do something crazy. Can you partner with me to do all this work and do it for free?" Origin Protocol had already built an Ethereum-powered platform to bring NFTs to the masses, and luckily, they said yes.

The project was a perfect storm, and its success was due to the buy-in of the artists and the collectors coupled with the excitement of a historical event raising funds for a world-renowned children's hospital.

Kyle was inspired by St. Jude's, and after the success of the first project, he offered to advise the team about blockchain and the types of things they could do. On the anniversary of their first collaboration, he came up with the idea to secure an .eth address that allows people to connect their digital wallets directly with a brand or an organization. People can donate what they want when they want to study .eth in the form of NFTs, Bitcoin, Ethereum, and other cryptocurrencies. This provided the hospital with an evergreen fundraising opportunity, as giving doesn't need to center around a particular launch, drop, or event.

What's Next?

Kyle acknowledges that the NFT space is experimental, and the team at Subtractive is learning as they go. They are working with brands and sharing their experiences to help others avoid the mistakes they made early in the process.

Ultimately, if what you are doing checks out with your community, if it is authentic and feels like the right thing, it probably is the right thing. Being authentic involves collecting, supporting, going to events, sponsoring events, showing up, listening instead of talking, hearing what the community needs, and helping them get it. Or finding artists that might be underrepresented and helping them get somewhere selflessly. This is what's most important.

Everyone needs to make money, but in this space, what you give is what you get, and if you come from a place of giving, you'll thrive in the community and have a chance of success. The tech is not quite there yet, but when it is, mass adoption will come.

Clutch Wallet

CRYPTO and WEB3

The crypto wallet is an essential part of the emerging NFT and Web3 ecosystem, as it serves as a hub for all of your digital assets, including your capital, purchases, and even your identity. As Web3 technology continues to develop, it is likely that your crypto wallet will become increasingly important and integrated into your online presence. The phrase "Connect your wallet" could even become a common way to share contact information, similar to how people currently use phrases like "tweet me" or "email me."

Bec Jones, CEO and co-founder of Clutch Wallet[50], is working to provide education, insight, and information on Web3 for first-time users, with a particular focus on women. She is using platforms like TikTok to share her message and gather feedback and market intelligence from her more than 50k followers. By offering a user-friendly and accessible way to learn about and engage with the Web3 ecosystem, Bec and the team at Clutch Wallet are helping to pave the way for wider adoption and understanding of this exciting new technology.

Use Case

Bec Jones, Clutch Wallet co-founder and lead on marketing and community, has spent the last four years in the crypto industry working across various projects and managing communities (Vid and Anon).

Clutch Wallet's objective is not only to onboard and nurture women into a new wave of the Internet and finance but to reduce the wealth gap once they are on-boarded.

Clutch Wallet is building a cryptocurrency wallet with a mission to onboard the 81% of women who are yet to transact with cryptocurrencies. Clutch will be built on both web and mobile applications allowing users to hold, invest in, and trade digital assets on the Ethereum blockchain. We believe the current products built in the crypto industry, in particular - wallets, do not help first-time users, are confusing, badly designed, and do not create a sense of security or familiarity.

Clutch is focusing on partnering with women-focused crypto communities and brands launching into Web3. There is a huge opportunity to bring Web2 users into Web3 through NFTs and first investments into crypto. Clutch Wallet plans to nurture that first-time experience by offering not only gamified education (learn and earn) but social wallet features as well.

Women have traditionally been left out of emerging markets, particularly in the finance and money industries. Web3 promotes equality for all with access and opportunity to invest and participate in a financial market and new stage of the Internet. Unfortunately, adoption of this new industry's technologies is still low, with many people, in particular women, citing it as confusing, overwhelming, supported by bro culture, and not inclusive. Women, in particular, are currently banding together to invest as a collective through DAOs, participate in NFT drops and learn/engage as a community (discord channels, telegram groups, Facebook groups).

Some of the data Clutch cares about includes:

- Women own $0.32c to the $1 that men own in the United States, black women owning only $0.1c- Ellevest
- 1.7 billion unbanked individuals across the world. 1B of those individuals are women - World bank global finance index
- 81% of women globally are yet to interact/invest in cryptocurrencies - TIME Magazine

Clutch is focusing on creating a digital wallet experience that not only facilitates basic wallet functions like buying, swapping, sending, and receiving cryptocurrencies but also allows users to educate themselves across a range of different crypto topics.

Clutch interviewed 636 women to understand their perceptions of crypto, investing, and the current wallet user experience. The following results were found:

- $38K sitting idle in savings accounts
- 73% of respondents said they would use a crypto wallet tailored to women
- 48% said they would spend $100-$1000 per month on average investing in crypto
- 81% of respondents said they would like to invest their money into crypto
- 65% said, "I don't understand it", which is stopping them from investing in crypto
- 79% said a "more user-friendly/simple UX" is important to them when using a crypto wallet

Spiral is a company that builds and funds free, open-source projects aimed at making Bitcoin the planet's preferred currency. They recently conducted research into understanding how women outside the US who never engaged with Bitcoin felt about it and how their perceptions differed from men's. The following highlights:

- Global attitudes towards Bitcoin are essentially the same across genders
- Women need to do more research than men before deciding to purchase Bitcoin.
- More women than men consider themselves "very comfortable" taking financial risks
- Facebook, YouTube, and Instagram are the preferred platforms for women and men who want to learn about Bitcoin

All of this data demonstrates that there is a unique opportunity for women, and they do have a risk appetite and are interested in participating in Web3. Since August of 2021, with the introduction of World of Women NFT, we have seen strong growth in women investing together, as communities, in NFT collections and digital fashion brands that resonate and matter to them. Clutch recognizes there are nuances to creating diverse products which suit the needs and interests of different groups.

In particular, Clutch is excited to support the population of 'unbanked' opening a non-custodial cryptocurrency wallet that only requires an email address to activate. Globally in 2022, 1.7 billion people remain unbanked, and 1 billion of those people are women. The world of Web3 has many job opportunities for work online/in communities that can help people work and earn a living with payments made in crypto.

The NFT and crypto industry is one of the fastest-growing industries in the market. The introduction of NFTs, and in particular in the profile picture space, has just scratched the surface of what utility can be held in utilizing blockchain to represent ownership in the digital world. As a wallet provider, we are beyond excited to support people leaning into Web3, owning their own assets, building wealth, and participating in the future of the Internet.

References:

- https://time.com/nextadvisor/investing/cryptocurrency/women-in-crypto/
- https://twitter.com/spiralbtc/status/1519671312930725888?s=20&t=WpgIaizJzPR-d2-o5b27Hw

Chapter 5

Imagine That - Ready Player *YOU*

As Web3 and the metaverse continue to evolve, we can expect to see more partnerships and collaborations between established institutions and emerging technology companies. For example, the Parsons School of Design[51] has partnered with Roblox to offer a course on digital fashion design using the platform's tools. While there are still many challenges to be addressed in the development of the metaverse, such as governance and user interface, the potential for creativity and exploration like this collaboration is immense.

Elements of the movie Ready Player One[52], such as commercial space travel, autonomous vehicles, altered states, virtual realities, new currencies, and extremely advanced artificial intelligence, are becoming a reality. Whether it's a new version of the metaverse or the Nike version, or what some have referred to as the multiverse (multiple connected metaverse spaces), the future is coming.

With these developments will be Ready Player **YOU**. What will it look like? What will you look like? How will it work? What will you do there?

It is up to each of us to shape and create the virtual reality spaces we want to explore and interact with. The possibilities are endless, and the creativity and desire to explore these new lands are compelling.

Here's what mega consulting firm <u>Deloitte says</u>[53], "The Metaverse in 2040. *"Hype? Hope? Hell? Maybe all three. Experts are split about the likely evolution of a truly immersive 'metaverse.' They expect that augmented- and mixed-reality enhancements will become more useful in people's daily lives. Many worry that current online problems may be magnified if Web3 development is led by those who built today's dominant web platforms."* Deloitte 2022

While the future of the metaverse is still unknown, Deloitte goes on to list several actions executives can take now:

Don't underestimate the potential: Formulate a metaverse strategy but keep it flexible enough to adapt to changes in technology and consumer preferences. Adopt a "test and learn" approach for both consumer-facing and enterprise functions.

Take the long view: Given the mainstream metaverse and corresponding revenue generation are likely several years out, companies should take a long-term view on investments and consider KPIs around consumer and employee engagement in addition to ROI. Consider investments in the context of broader digital transformation agendas.

Focus on demand and what motivates users: Organizations should focus on how to create captivating content and engaging experiences (e.g., exclusive partnerships, user-generated content tools, robust data, and insights collection) in order to establish share and remain competitive.

Commit to a "responsible metaverse": Organizations will need to manage a range of complexities and risks in the metaverse (e.g., privacy/security, accessibility, sustainable energy consumption) and ensure they are proactively building a responsible metaverse and effectively maintaining consumer and employee trust.

Good guidance. In order to effectively navigate the shift to Web3 and the next phase of digital transformation, companies will need leaders who understand the broader implications of these changes and can develop a business strategy that is aligned with the advent of new technologies.

In addition to the growth of the digital world, we also see a broader shift in societal attitudes and perspectives, which I have referred to as the *Great ReThink*. As we move into 2023 and beyond, more and more people recognize that virtual reality and real-life reality can coexist and are both equally valid.

At the same time, many of the fundamental tasks and activities of our everyday lives, such as working, raising children, and caring for loved ones, will continue to be important. It is likely that we will need to develop new skills and adapt to new technologies in order to continue functioning in both the digital and real-world 'multiverses'. The rise of robotics and automation will surely play a role in this shift. Ultimately, the future of the virtual multiverse is still uncertain, and it will be important to continue to adapt and evolve as it continues to develop.

How will YOU react to these changes? Juggling multiple realities should not be new news. It has been coming for over 10+ years. Millions of people are living in real life (IRL) and virtually at the same time already. They are live streamers, gamers, social media users, and Gen Alpha on Roblox. In addition, during the pandemic, Zoom showed the entire world that a digital presence could and does coexist with an IRL presence.

I wrote about data analytics, virtual currencies, and "artificial reality" (now augmented reality) 11 years ago in my first book. It took five additional years for the social media world to talk about data analytics seriously and another 3-5 years for anyone to talk about virtual currencies as a 'thing'. These topics are the true 'meta', in my opinion, because they underlie everything that is happening now and will happen for the next 5-10 years. This is the Meta of the metaverse.

These topics were intriguing to me then and even more now. Blockchain languished a bit after its ICO bubble burst in 2017. It is now back with a big bang. Back in 2018, we did a blockchain concept analysis for Lamborghini, a legendary brand client. Way before our time. We were recommending tokenizing assets at that time, in addition to enterprise blockchain. That was much harder to conceive of and to do then. NFTs were not even on the horizon for most. And now, here we are, in 2023.

New Leadership and Inspiration

One of the key principles of Web3 is that it empowers individuals and communities to take control of their own data and online identities. This opens up new possibilities for leadership and inspiration in a way that was not possible before.

As we've seen, Web3 is inspiring new forms of leadership in the realm of online communities. Decentralized social networks, forums, and other online platforms are allowing individuals to come together and create their own rules and governance structures. This is empowering people to take ownership of their online spaces and to create communities that are more inclusive and diverse.

Web3 is also enabling new forms of collaboration and coordination among individuals and organizations. For example, decentralized autonomous organizations (DAOs) allow groups of people to come together and make collective decisions without the need for a central authority. This is inspiring a new generation of leaders who are able to coordinate complex projects and initiatives in a way that was not possible before.

Overall, Web3 is fostering a new era of leadership and inspiration in which individuals and communities are empowered to take control of their own data, identities, and online spaces. This is leading to the creation of more diverse and equitable online communities and enabling people to collaborate and coordinate in new and exciting ways.

BigTech Becomes YouTech

As we become more aware of how BigTech and BigSocial companies manipulate us through their Web2 algorithms by collecting and using our data and content for their own purposes, it is important for individuals to now take responsibility for their own privacy and security. We have the power to define our own digital identities and to make informed choices about how we present ourselves online and in real life. We are also responsible for our own money, whether it is digital or fiat, and it is up to us to be smart and vigilant in protecting ourselves from misinformation, disinformation, and manipulation.

Technology can be a powerful tool for us to connect, share information, and be more productive, but it is important to remember that we have the ability to make it work for us rather than allowing ourselves to be controlled by it. We still have the ability to reach thousands, or even millions, of people practically for free, and we have access to more information than ever before. AI can help us be more efficient and effective in our work, but it is up to us to use it responsibly and ethically.

Consumers are not off the hook, however. Yes, new creative tools are emerging, and you get to define who you are and how you roll. At the same time, it is the individual's responsibility to pay attention and create a society that values trust and truth once again. I'll leave the particulars to social scientists, but say again – YOU are in charge of your privacy and security.

YOU are in charge of how you present digitally and IRL. YOU are responsible for your money – digital and/or fiat. YOU are responsible for YOU. Continue to be smart about it – yes, the algorithms and social engineering are real and can be highly manipulative and dangerous. Misinformation and disinformation are happening ON PURPOSE. You are the target. Your data, your choices, and your beliefs are the target. Guard those as you would guard your life.

Make technology work for you. We still have the ability to reach thousands, millions even, practically for free. We have more information at our fingertips than ever before. AI can and will actually help us be more productive, especially if ethics and policies are written in.

Right now, new companies are forming that leverage these new technologies. There is excitement in the air. The future can be bright, and you can decide how you will participate.

The Ownership Economy is Here

Digital transformation was a theme in both large multinational corporations and small businesses a few years before the pandemic, say from 2015 – 2019. Then time stopped in March 2020, and interesting developments occurred around the business environment. Those companies that were well into their 'digital transformation' were situated to meet the new challenge. Those that had merely been paying lip service to digital transformation were way behind the eight-ball, and it showed.

With the whole world suddenly reliant on Zoom, we learned who was where on this transformation map. In some cases, whole industries leapfrogged about a decade of apathy in terms of advancement. Healthcare found out that 'telehealth', in fact, worked, *and* patients and doctors liked the convenience. Businesses found out that workers *can* be productive at work and at home, creating the 'work/life balance consultants have been touting for years. Parents found out that teachers really do work hard and that teaching is not as easy as it might look. Higher education found itself in the midst of a reckoning in terms of value delivered vs. cost. And we all learned that content is, in fact, king. And that it matters but not necessarily in the ways we once thought. The business of entertainment content really had some soul-searching to do, as did sports and media. And so on.

Companies are looking to provide the right mix of virtual plus IRL while workers are determining if they are in the right job for them after all or if they might be happier doing something else, somewhere else.

We will get through this adjustment period, sometimes not so gracefully, but we'll pull through. The big question is,

Now What? What do we want our company and/or brand to look like going forward? And what new companies, technologies, and methodologies should we be looking at? What will YOU do?

Magnitude of Change

Just as the industrial economy was wildly different from the agrarian, the Ownership Economy and Web3 is a radical departure from the way we've done business for the last 100 years. We can no longer rely on assumptions about processes, products, and customer behavior. If the last generation of software was built upon a foundation of *user-generated* content, the next generation of software would be *user-owned* content, with digital ownership leveraged as a building block to enable novel user experiences.

At its core, the ownership economy not only offers a powerful new tool for builders to leverage market incentives to jumpstart new networks—it also holds the potential to create positive social change through the wider distribution of wealth-building assets.

NFTs and Web3 are About Culture, not Technology

While technology is certainly a driving force behind the emergence of NFTs and the growth of the Web3 ecosystem, it is important to recognize that these developments are also about culture. Culture shapes the way we think about and interact with technology, and it plays a critical role in determining the ways in which new technologies are adopted and integrated into our lives.

The cultural impacts of NFTs and Web3 are wide-ranging and complex, and they touch on everything from art and entertainment to finance and social interaction. The decentralized nature of Web3 technology, for example, has the potential to disrupt traditional power structures and enable new forms of social and economic exchange. At the same time, the rise of the metaverse and the development of virtual reality spaces have the potential to change the way we think about identity, community, and human interaction.

Ultimately, the success of NFTs and Web3 will depend on our ability to adapt and embrace these technologies in a way that aligns with our cultural values and goals. This will require a purposeful and continuous effort to manage and shape the cultural impacts of these technologies and to ensure that they are used in a way that benefits society as a whole.

The Great ReThink

From March 2020 to right now, people around the world have been rethinking just about every aspect of their lives. How we work, what's important, how we deal with mental health, how we travel, how we spend our time, what brings value, what gives pleasure, where to live, who to love, how to be informed, who to trust, and so on. What have YOU been rethinking?

Many are also rethinking what motivates and what inspires them. During the pandemic, celebrities and influencers suddenly didn't seem to have quite the same glow or the sheen they once had. Things they do or say in troubled times can disappoint their fans. It turns out that (surprise!) they are just like us in so many ways, which may be even more disappointing to some.

We somehow want those we admire in media, sports, entertainment, politics, and religion to be superhuman, to never have faults, and to always stay in character. Or at least that's what we've been doing for the past 30+ years. The upside of the Great ReThink is that collectively we seem to value authenticity more than ever, and somehow knowing our 'heroes' are human beings too can be comforting.

Politics, education, government, fame, fortune, common courtesy, empathy – it seems like everything is upended. Everything is fallible, and nothing is what we once thought it was. Some believe this is a good thing – time to rearrange the universe, so to speak. Others see dystopia, fear, and anger. There's no going back, that is for sure. If it feels like the social contracts we've had with one another are broken, it is because, in many ways, they have been.

The rules have changed for personal relations, business, communication, and the way everyone uses and values their time. Few are inspired by downers. Don't be that downer who's never curious, always complaining, and poking holes in everything. It's important to be realistic about what is underfoot. It is also important to remember there is almost always a silver lining somewhere.

Be the Bright Spot

How can you, your brand, or your company make someone's day better? How do you present when you are with clients, customers, and groups that you are involved in? What inspires that group? How can you add to that?

Yes, it's scary out there. We live in a tech surveillance world. There is little privacy. Your data is valuable, but you don't profit from it. It could all go the wrong way, and often does. Authoritarian views seem to be appealing to some in times like these. Squid Game is one of the most watched shows ever. A dystopian apocalypse could be around the corner.

OR NOT.

We just don't know. Sixty years ago, kids in America practiced regular 'duck and cover' exercises to prepare for a coming nuclear war. People built bomb shelters in their basements. No one was going to get out alive, though. That was the 'certainty' the population lived with.

This is not to minimize the threats all around us, real or imagined. Climate change, space wars, scarce resources, disrupted supply chains or no supply chains at all, disinformation, controversies, World War III, and crypto scams... could all swallow us up any minute.

But this is now Ready Player YOU. Every day, you, as an individual, have a choice. Life goes on. Look for opportunities and forge onward. In the midst of all that's scary could be the seeds for something better. I choose to operate that way. I ask myself, "What's great about what's happening now? Clarity is power. How can I either maximize or learn from this situation?"

We All Need to Be Inspired

At times like these, inspiration can sometimes seem fleeting and far away. It feels fake or like a luxury for another time. Where does inspiration come from, anyhow?

Inspiration seems to occur spontaneously, without intention. It's likely to feel like something that happens *to* you rather than something that you choose or plan to experience. I would say this is mostly true. I love it when something –

music, art, writing, a speech, or nature – inspires me. It's like a gift – there it is, out of nowhere! It feels special and can make me feel special.

It *is* also possible to choose and plan to look for inspiration and create inspiration for you and others. This is up to you. You can wait to be inspired, and/or you can search for inspiration. Both are possible.

You can wait for others to light the fire. You can complain about this and that, and woe is me. The world is different; whatever will I do? Or you can choose to step up in some way that is authentic to you, and that then inspires others. That's how you thrive in the digital age and in virtual worlds.

Think of something that absolutely had an inspirational impact on you - a speech, a performance, something in nature that is breathtaking, a moving moment with another, a brilliant idea sparked by chance. WHAT was it that inspired you? Try to re-live that experience in detail and identify the inspirational elements – a tone of voice, ideas expressed, and vision created. Inspiration is exhilarating, and yet it is not something that can be manufactured or taught. But we can seek inspiration and, sometimes, find it.

I am inspired by my students. I am inspired by young people entering STEAM programs and inventing and developing our future. I am inspired by entrepreneurs with big ideas. I am inspired by my younger family members. I am often inspired by music and art – think about what it takes to be that creative! I am deeply inspired by emerging technology. Not just the technology itself but what it means, what it enables, and what might happen as a result of the new developments. I am inspired by the spirit of the universe.

The current Web3 and NFT developments are extremely inspirational to me... and to many others. I am inspired by these new developments, and I have been researching and immersing myself in this new world *because* I am inspired. I hope to inspire some of you as well.

Yes, inspiration can be very elusive and fleeting, even in the best of times and often in the worst of times. But waiting to be inspired is a fool's game.

Now is the time to find inspiration, share that inspiration, and live an inspired life. This is strength. This is power. The ability to go on and see possibilities no matter what the circumstances – that is what YOU are capable of.

One of the highest compliments I've received is to be told that I am an inspiration to others. Wow, thank you! I have thought about this quite a bit and want to share some observations with you that may help you in this virtual age.

Inspiration is about to move to a whole new level with NFTs and Web3. Just the fact that they exist is inspirational. On top of that, the creativity and world of possibilities about to descend upon us all is massively inspirational.

I challenge my students, and I'll challenge you to put some thought into inspiration and why it matters – to you, to business, and to the world. I advise each one to find something that inspires them and hold on to it. This has never been more important. So, shut out the naysayers. Yes, it's hard out there in many ways. Out of chaos, an opportunity is created. Be the inspiration, find the opportunity, share it, and then live it.

Thriving in the digital and virtual age will require that you are able to both find inspiration and be inspirational. The great thing about the digital age and virtual worlds is that they give everyone a voice. The downside to this is that it is very noisy and chaotic. I've seen really good ideas and plans meander off into nothing due to the noise level. This happens when there is a lack of inspiration and leadership.

This is an excellent time for some to choose to step forward as leaders. Choosing a leadership role can be exhilarating and terrifying at the same time. Much is written about leadership – what it is, what it means, and how to develop leadership qualities. I encourage you to look into the topic, find TED talks on leadership, podcasts on what makes a good leader, etc. Learn all you can and think it over, even if you don't feel it applies to you. There is always something you can glean from gathering knowledge about a subject.

Leaders take responsibility for their actions. Lately, however, we've seen a lack of leaders in business, governments, religions, etc., willing to take responsibility for their actions. In my opinion, this is a real tragedy. Don't fall into that category. Don't follow leaders who can just give good speeches and get everyone fired up in the short term. Find those who choose leadership qualities that are lasting – that are committed and inspirational.

Inspired leaders are inspirational. They encourage and empower others to find their unique qualities and be that leader that acts with independently accountable passion in their own right. They have a vision that aligns with the group's core values. They motivate, manage, and support their teams to work creatively and confidently toward that shared vision.

Web3 and NFTs are accelerating at an increased pace every day. You need to know your value and be able to communicate how it can be useful in any given situation. Be the person who sees new possibilities instead of dread and darkness. Yes, be realistic, and then turn your attention to how to transcend and help others transcend. Move into possibility.

Find Inspiration

What inspires you? Take a minute and write down right now five things and/or people that inspire you. What about them has been inspirational to you? Be as detailed as possible.

If this was hard for you, you've got work to do. You've got to *find inspiration*. It is critical to keep the fire lit and motivate you to take that next step. The Great ReThink has really made this evident. The search for meaning, for motivation, for inspiration was never more evident than during the pandemic.

It is your job to find what motivates YOU. It can be as simple as the joy you get when you see your pets or your children, or other loved ones. It can be a cause near and dear to your heart. It can be a favorite song or melody, a favorite film or film character, art and artwork, a favorite sports team or athlete, or nature in all its glory. It can be a feeling, it can be an idea, it can be quiet, or it can be loud. Whatever it is, look for it and figure out what attributes are inspirational to you.

I once heard a wise person say that everyone was asking him about finding happiness. His advice was to go make a list of 50 things that make you happy and then come back after you complete the list.

I took that challenge. I was excited to list, finally, what would make me truly happy. I got to about 32 items on my list and started to falter. It was hard to list 50 things I genuinely thought would make me happy. When I completed my list, I returned to find out the next step.

His next piece of advice was simple and profound. He said, "Now go DO all of those things on your list, and you will be happy."

An important lesson here. Don't wait for inspiration to magically appear. Identify what inspires you, and then go do those things. If mountain climbing is inspirational to you – go do that – and maybe invent a way to do that in the virtual world. If a specific cause or charity is meaningful to you, find out how you can add value and how you can contribute. If your children inspire you, spend more time with them. And so on. Passion is exhilarating, and most inspirational people are passionate about something. Find yours.

Share Inspiration

Inspirational people share their inspiration with others. It's infectious. They are able to tell the story, create the scene, and explain the cause in a way that gets you thinking. It puts you right there and can spread enthusiasm and make you want to sign up right now. Something happens when others rally around a great idea or cause. The momentum takes over, and everyone begins to move in the same direction.

As we emerge from the pandemic and its associated mindset and lifestyle, there is an opportunity for individuals to step forward as leaders and active participants in their families, communities, schools, and workplaces. Rather than waiting for others to take the lead, we can take on the challenge of inspiring and motivating those around us to work towards a shared vision.

By learning how to manage and support teams in a way that fosters creativity and confidence, we can empower team members to embrace their own unique leadership qualities and act with independently accountable passion. We can also inspire and motivate teams to maintain long-term progress and excitement as they work towards achieving their goals.

Now is the time to seize the opportunity to be a leader and make a positive impact in the world. Whether it's in your personal life or in your professional career, there are always ways to inspire and empower those around you to achieve their full potential. By embracing your own leadership qualities and acting with purpose, you can make a lasting difference in the lives of others and the world around you.

Live Inspiration

Every so often, people say to me, "You are so inspirational". Thank you, but what exactly does that mean? I got to thinking about living an inspired life. It's easy to envision some idealized picture of the shining light on the hill, etc. I am a realist. I have no problem admitting the true state of things. I love strategic thinking, and that always starts with an accurate assessment of the current state – the good, the bad, and the ugly. Where are we today? Where am I today? Where are my company, my group, my family, and my kids today? And where do we want to go – what is our end point? Then we can think about how to get there.

Living an inspirational life, in my view, requires this type of assessment. Look around, and things are in flux in many ways right now. Take another look at all the innovation and new thinking all around YOU. Think of a baby born right now – their life is just beginning, and the possibilities are truly endless. In spite of the current state, great things can and will happen. Why not be a part of that instead of being part of the doom and gloom? Or, use the gloomy parts of the world to inspire you to take action and get others to take action.

To truly live a life that inspires others, it's important to take the things that inspire you and make them a central part of your daily existence. This isn't about trying to be a cheerleader in the face of difficult challenges or crises but rather about being genuine and authentic in your actions and intentions. At the same time, it's important to recognize that inspiration isn't always easy or constant and that it's okay to have moments of struggle or difficulty.

One way to inspire and give hope to others is by sharing your own experiences and how you got through rough times. This can be especially powerful if you're able to provide practical advice or strategies that others can use to overcome their own challenges.

To be an effective leader with vision and the ability to empower others to achieve their best, it's important to focus on execution and take concrete steps toward achieving your goals. This might involve finding inspiring guest speakers or seeking out new opportunities to connect with others and share your ideas. By working hard to bring your best effort to everything you do and helping others to do the same, you can inspire and motivate those around you to live lives they can be proud of.

Not the End But Another Beginning

Our flock of birds continues to form and dart and separate in an endless flow. That is the way of nature and the way of this world. From PCs to NFTs - we are embarking on a new cycle in this endless flow – one that promises to be truly game-changing. I know that I am inspired, and I hope this book has inspired you as well.

Becoming inspired is a powerful and transformative experience. It can give us a sense of purpose and direction and can motivate us to achieve great things. Becoming inspired often requires a shift in perspective. This means looking at the world with fresh eyes and seeing things in a new light.

As you continue on your journey and explore the possibilities of NFTs and Web3, I encourage you to imagine yourself as a part of this new renaissance in whatever way resonates with you and your brand or company. Whether you're an artist, a collector, an entrepreneur, or simply someone who is interested in these technologies, there are countless ways to get involved and make a positive impact.

I have no doubt that you will be amazed by the possibilities and the potential for creative expression and innovation. I encourage you to stay open to new ideas, embrace change, and be bold in the pursuit of your goals.

Onward and upward, and I look forward to seeing you in the next world. Don't be late!

Understanding Intellectual Property in NFTs

By Natalia Aranovich, Esq.

Intellectual Property is so vitally important in the world of creativity and NFTs, and also to the general education of the public. Deep acknowledgment to Natalia de Campos Aranovich, Esq., who specializes in Intellectual Property, for generously contributing this very comprehensive view on NFTs and IP. It is of such great importance, and the purpose of including it is to help educate the reader.

*Disclaimer – **THIS IS NOT LEGAL ADVICE***

WHAT ARE YOU BUYING AND SELLING?
NFTs, INTELLECTUAL PROPERTY, AND SMART CONTRACTS:
BASIC LEGAL DEFINITIONS FOR NON-LAWYERS

"NFTs" is short for non-fungible tokens, and they have been the new buzzword in the market since 2021. Many people feel like outsiders in this new world of NFTs, especially those who have never owned one, minted one, or even know what one is altogether. This new era of Web3 has been called the era of "owning your own IP", and people are learning how to monetize their IP on the web by using NFTs. Thus, before you start selling and/or buying NFTs, you should understand what they are, what is behind them, and what are their legal implications of them related to intellectual property issues.

I.   **WHAT ARE NFTs?**

NFTs are digital data (referred to as tokens) that certify that something is authentic and unique on the Internet. The certification, which the NFT represents, is connected to a physical or digital asset, such as a painting, digital artwork, music, movie, photograph, article of clothing, collectible, etc. You buy NFTs with a digital currency called "cryptocurrency," which is stored in a wallet. The most popular digital currency for purchasing NFTs until now has been Ethereum, but there are others. NTFs are available online for purchase on websites such as open sea (www.opensea.com[54]) and others. When we say an NFT represents a unique asset, it means that the NFT certifies that something is non-fungible and that it cannot be exchanged for another of the same kind. For example, one of Van Gogh's paintings is non-fungible because there is only one Van Gogh painter and one of that specific paintings painted by Van Gogh. On the other hand, money is fungible because you can exchange a $5 bill for another $5 bill. Thus, when we say someone owns an NFT, it means that he/she owns the asset exclusively, and there is no other original available for sale.

People like to compare NFTs to a deed. For example, when you buy a house, if you just sign the purchase agreement, you do not own the house or have the property yet. The deed needs to be recorded in order for you to own the house/have the property. Then, once the deed is recorded, you have proof that you own the house/property. However, the deed itself is not the house or the property. It is just proof of ownership. Additionally, once you have the deed, only you own the house, and there are not two of those houses identical for sale on that same land. The same occurs with NFTs. Once you own the NFT, you have proof of ownership of the physical or digital asset that the NFT certifies is authentic and unique, but the NFT is not the digital or physical asset itself.

In order to buy or sell an NFT, the first thing you need is a wallet to safeguard the cryptocurrency you purchase. You can have a centralized or noncentralized wallet. The difference between the two is that a third party controls a centralized wallet, meaning if you lose the password to your wallet, you can contact that third party to try to access it. A noncentralized wallet, on the other hand, does not have a company or an individual behind the wallet, which means there is no one to contact if you lose your credentials to access it. Thus, if you lose your key to a noncentralized wallet, you can say goodbye to your cryptocurrency.

After you have a wallet, you then need to "mint" your digital file on a website to generate a token (NFT) and put it up for sale on a blockchain. When you put your digital or physical asset up for sale as an NFT, you must also create a "smart contract" for it that specifies the terms of the sale: i.e., how the purchaser can use your NFT, if there are any intellectual property rights connected to it, royalties, etc.

NFTs are evolving fast, and lawyers are trying to understand the legal consequences of their use and exactly what underlying rights are connected to them. There are several legal definitions for digital assets related to NFTs. For example, the IRS describes them as property, and FinCEN describes them as currency. However, notwithstanding those legal definitions, this paper will discuss only the intellectual property issues related to NFTs.

II. WHAT IS INTELLECTUAL PROPERTY, AND HOW DOES IT RELATE TO NFTs?

The relationship between intellectual property (IP) and NFTs is important to consider when you are buying and/or selling digital or real (that exist in the real world) assets that contain images and brands. For example, IP laws might not be relevant if you are buying and/or selling real estate (real property) through an NFT. However, they are important if you are buying and/or selling a digital or physical image, a digital good that contains a trademark on it, or a drawing or image that is protected by copyright or trademark laws through an NFT.

In short, IP is an idea created by the human mind that is protected by the law. It can be something you write or create, a name for your product or service, secret business information you know, or an invention. Thus, IP is the protection of ideas in the legal world. However, not all ideas are protected in the legal world. Let's first explore what ideas can be protected through IP law, including copyrights (what you write or create), trademarks (the name of your products or services), patents (inventions), and trade secrets (something you know that is unique to your business).

To begin, if I buy a painting in the physical world, that painting is protected by IP Laws and, more specifically, by copyright laws. This means I own the painting, and I can place it whenever I would like, but I cannot copy the painting and make reproductions of it for sale to the public because I don't own the copyright. The same thinking process should be applied when you buy a digital image certificated through an NFT, meaning you will own the digital image. However, the fact that you own the digital image does not mean that you can make copies of it and start selling reproductions of it in other places without the authorization of the copyright holder. Such authorization must be in writing and probably will be in terms of the smart contract associated with the NFT. For that reason, it is important when buying and/or selling NFTs to first determine whether you are buying and/or selling only the asset or the asset with some or all IP rights associated with it. In order to learn what IP rights you are buying and/or selling, you will need to read the terms of the smart contract associated with the NFT. It is the smart contract that will define the terms of the sale, including whether you have or will license or transfer the copyright of the intellectual property that is certified by the NFT.

Considering that, let's now dive into the basic definitions of the different types of intellectual property and see how they relate to NFTs.

Copyrights

Copyrights protect original works of authorship (something you write or create) expressed in a tangible form (something you can see, touch, or hear). If you own a copyright, that means you have the exclusive right to copy the work, create new works based on the existing work, distribute the work to others, publicly perform the work, publicly display the work, and license or transfer the rights. These rights are bestowed upon the owner once the copyrightable work is created, whether the owner registers it with the U.S. Copyright Office or not. Registration is not necessary for one to have the copyright. However, without registration with the U.S. Copyright Office, the owner of a copyrightable work loses some rights related to the copyright laws, including (public notice, statutory damages, attorney's fees and costs, and file a lawsuit for copyright infringement). To apply for copyright protection with the Copyright Office, you can do it by yourself at www.copyright.gov or seek the help of an attorney.

Not all original ideas are copyrightable. They must be "fixed in a tangible medium of expression," which means you can see and/or touch and/or hear the work. Additionally, the work must be created by a human. Some examples of copyrightable works include books, artwork, pictures, photographs, drawings, paintings, sculptures, writings, music, videos, choreography, and more. In regards to NFTs, we could argue that a digital artwork or image sold through an NFT is an idea protected by copyright law if it fulfills the legal requirements explained above. If digital artwork and images certified by NFTs are considered "original ideas fixed in a tangible medium of expression," then we could potentially have a work that is copyright protected.

As described above, copyrights are important because they give the owner the exclusive right to sell, distribute copies, and license or transfer the right. Thus, when buying and/or selling work that is protected by copyright law, it is important to be aware of exactly what you are buying: i.e., the copyright itself or a limited right to use the work in a specific manner, such as the painting described above.

In the NFT world, two recent cases regarding copyrights and digital images are important to the discussion: *Miramax LLC v. Tarantino et al.*[1] (which is about copyright infringement and NFTs) and the U.S. Copyright Review

---

[1] *Miramax LLC v. Tarantino et al*, C.D. Cal., No. 2:21-cv-08979, 11/16/21

Board's Refusal to Register A Recent Entrance to Paradise (which is about copyright and artificial intelligence).[2]

Copyright Infringement and NFTs

In November 2021, Quentin Tarantino, the director of the cult classic *Pulp Fiction*, announced a planned sale of NFTs based on his original hand-written script of *Pulp Fiction*. Tarantino's website displayed the following: "each NFT consists of a single iconic scene, including personalized audio commentary from Quentin Tarantino. The collector who purchases one of these few and rare NFTs will get a hold of secrets from the screenplay and a glimpse into the mind and the creative process of Quentin Tarantino. The owner [of the NFT] will enjoy the freedom of choosing between: "keeping the secrets to him/herself or sharing them."[3]

Shortly after Tarantino's announcement, Miramax, the studio that produced the 1994 hit film, filed a lawsuit in California, alleging, among others, copyright infringement. Miramax's claim asserts that its ownership of its copyright of *Pulp Fiction* included the finished film and "all elements in thereof in all stages of development and production."[4] Tarantino argues that his NFTs contain content outside of the scope of Miramax's copyright ownership in *Pulp Fiction*, or alternatively, that his use is fair use.

---

[2]https://www.copyright.gov/rulings-filings/review-board/docs/a-recent-entrance-to-paradise.pdf

[3]https://tarantinonfts.com/

[4]https://www.lexology.com/library/detail.aspx?g=b87fd36d-e26d-41d2-aed5-4f408f5bcb50&utm_source=Lexology+Daily+Newsfeed&utm_medium=HTML+email+...

This case was settled in September2022 but the dispute between Tarantino and Miramax highlights two major problems in the NFT world today. First, it is unclear who has the right to sell NFTs in the first place. In this case, this was established in a previous written contract between the parties that needs to be interpreted. Second, courts have yet to establish ways to rectify unlawful NFTs if it is determined that a person without rights sold one. This case is important because it may be the first to address who has the right to create an NFT, any legal significance of an NFT, and whether artists have residual rights to their content.

Copyright and Artificial Intelligence

On November 3, 2018, Steven Thaler ("Thaler") filed an application for a U.S. copyright registration of a digital image ("Image") called "A Recent Entrance to Paradise." In the application, Thaler identified "Creativity Machine" as the author of the work and not himself. He also stated that the Image was "autonomously created by a computer algorithm running on a machine" and that he was seeking to register the Image as a "work-for-hire to the owner of the Creative Machine."

On August 12, 2019, the US Copyright Office refused Thaler's registration, stating that the Image "lack[ed] the human authorship necessary to support a copyright claim." In response, Thaler filed a request for reconsideration on the grounds that the "human authorship requirement [was] unconstitutional and unsupported by either statute or case law," an argument which the Copyright Office rejected. Thaler subsequently filed a second request for reconsideration, largely repeating the same arguments in his first, which again was rejected by the Copyright Office in the current decision at issue herein.

In summary, the Copyright Office maintained its longstanding position that "the term authorship implies that, for a work to be copyrightable, it must owe its origins to a human being. Materials produced solely by nature, by plants, or by animals are not copyrightable." In their refusals of Thaler's requests, the Copyright Office also cited a USPTO decision about AI, saying that the author of a patent invention could not be the machine. There, the USPTO said that "the vast majority of comments acknowledged that existing laws does not permit non-human to be an author [and] this should remain the law." Finally, the Copyright Office also cited an important guideline from the COMPENDIUM (THIRD) §313.2., which explains that "the crucial question of human authorship is whether a computer is merely being an assisting instrument or actually conceive(s) and execute (s) the traditional elements of the work." Note that, in the decision of the registrability of the Image "A Recent Entrance to Paradise," the Copyright Office and Thaler are not discussing whether the computer that created the Image assisted in the creation of the Image or was self-executing. In Thaler's copyright application, he expressly stated that the Image was created by a "Creative Machine," meaning that it was self-executed by the computer. Thus, the Copyright Office applied its well-established understanding that non-humans cannot be the author of a copyrighted work. The decision also discusses the concept of work-for-hire, but that issue is not relevant for the purposes of this paper.

When the digital art movement started through the sale of NFTs, three main "digital art" collections gained notoriety in the NFT world: the CryptoPunks, the Bored Ape Yacht Club, and the CryptoKitties. There is not much literature on how those digital collectible images are created, but some research indicates that some of them could be created through an algorithm. The sale of those digital image collections is made through a smart contract attached to the digital image, allowing the "creator/author" to receive royalties each and every time they are purchased and resold on the Internet. However, there is not much discussion on whether those digital images could be copyrightable or the issue that was raised in the recent Copyright Office decision regarding "A Recent Entrance to Paradise" about the algorithm creating the image. If the same reasoning from the Copyright Office's recent decision is applicable to the digital image collections sold through NFTs that are created through algorithms, then the conclusion would be that they are not copyrightable and, as a result, you cannot attach the payment of "royalties" in a smart contract. Thinking alternatively, if these collections are not considered copyrightable, then perhaps they could be considered a simple product or an investment, although the latter of which could raise some securities law issues.

Lawyers are neither developers nor artists. However, the role of lawyers is not to code but rather to work with the law in order to solve problems for a client. With that said, one possible way to solve the issues regarding the sale of digital images as NFTs is to seek guidance from developers and artists alike to make sure that they understand the creative process behind the digital image. While the U.S Courts have yet to announce their view on the registrability of works created by algorithms as digital arts protected under the copyright law, the Copyright Office has some guidance saying that the crucial issue of images generated through an algorithm is whether the machine is merely assisting or conceiving and executing the elements of the work. Thus, it is also up to us lawyers to come up with arguments in favor or against the registrability of digital images created through algorithms or other AI mechanisms using this guidance.

The world has evolved, and so has the concept of how art is expressed. Before the Internet boom, visual artists used traditional mediums such as canvas, paper, pencils, paint, and other real tools to create their art. Now, in the modern world, and especially after the pandemic when everything became digital, art can be expressed through a computer as a digital image. The issue this raises, however, is whether that image generated by a computer through algorithms could be registered as a copyrightable work when the algorithm is only assisting the creator. From my point of view, we could follow two paths to try to answer that question.

The first path could be considering the concept of visual art and what the Copyright Office cited in the "A Recent Entrance to Paradise" decision: "the crucial question of human authorship is whether a computer is merely being an assisting instrument or actually conceive(s) and execute (s) the traditional elements of the work." As previously said, lawyers are not artists or coders themselves, but that doesn't mean they cannot try to understand. The second path could be looking at the code behind the digital image, which is a unique combination of words and numbers. Considering that the initial code is created by a human, could the code behind the digital image - the combination of words and numbers - be copyrightable as software? This is another interesting question to be answered.

These two paths are just two possible avenues to be discussed, though I suspect more will arise when lawyers begin to think outside the box, adapt to our new reality, and start thinking of new ideas to protect works created by and through new methods in the digital world. We must begin this discussion because digital art is here and likely going to be the future of art.

Remedy for Websites Selling NFTs if Copyright Infringement Exists: DMCA Takedown Notice

The Digital Millennium Copyright Act (DMCA) was signed into law by President Clinton on October 28, 1998, and establishes that websites displaying copyrighted material should have an email address or contact information for people to file claims regarding violations of the copyrighted material in the website.

As background, you are generally strictly liable for copyright infringement for infringing material hosted on your website, platform, or server, whether or not you know the material is there. DMCA Takedown Notices provide a "safe harbor" from liability to those entities that follow all the necessary statutory steps when third parties upload or post unauthorized copyrighted material to their platform, website, or server and (b) put a system in place for rights holders to have their unauthorized works removed efficiently. Entities that host infringing material on their platform, website, or server (even unwittingly) but fail to respond appropriately to a valid Take Down Notice lose their safe harbor from copyright infringement liability for the infringing material they are hosting and can face significant monetary damages.

The DMCA Take Down Notice should also be applicable when websites are selling NFTs that infringe on someone's copyright, and it is an important legal tool to be used by people selling NFTs using counterfeit content.

Trademarks

Trademarks are words, phrases, symbols, designs, smells (or a combination thereof) used to represent the name of goods or services of a business and differentiate them from others in the market. Some examples include Google for Internet search engine services, Apple for computer products, and Nike for sneakers. While trademarks are protected by common law at the state level without registration, there are benefits to registering your trademark with the U.S. Patent and Trademark Office (USPTO), including, but not limited to, the exclusive right to use the trademark nationwide. Considering that you do not need to register your trademark in order to have it, it is advisable that you register and, before using, conduct a search to make sure you won't use someone else's trademark. To register a trademark with the USPTO, you can do it by yourself at www.uspto.gov or seek the help of an attorney. Trademark registration procedures are not very easy, and if you decide to do it by yourself, make sure you understand all the procedures and codes needed for the application process.

You should choose a strong trademark to name your products and/or services. The stronger the trademark, the stronger the protection it has under trademark law. The strength of a trademark is determined by distinctiveness (see figure 1). According to the USPTO, fanciful, arbitrary, and suggestive words and phrases make the strongest trademarks because they are distinctive.

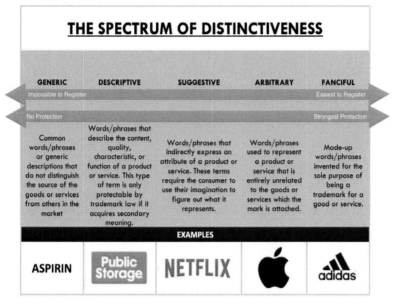

Figure 1: The Spectrum of Distinctiveness

Trademarks and NFTs

But, in the NFT world, what is the correlation between digital assets and trademarks? The digital assets behind NFTs are, at the basic level, products for sale to the public and, as such, have names that differentiate them from other digital assets in the market. For example, the BORED APE YACHT CLUB can be considered a trademark because it provides an Internet service for selling NFTs as digital art. CryptoPunks could also be considered a trademark. Additionally, as we discussed before, the drawing (digital art) of the CryptoPunk or other digital art sold through NFTs could be either copyrighted or trademarked or both. The images sold as CryptoPunks and the BORED APE YACHT CLUB have been associated with commercial use by the buyers. The smart contract allows them to make use of these images for commercial purposes under certain limitations. Thus, if someone decides to start a business selling mugs displaying those images, they are essentially "naming" their products and services, and the image becomes a trademark.

However, one should not confuse the image used to sell products and services with an image used to be displayed in a cartoon, for instance, which could be considered copyright. Let's continue to use the same image from the CryptoPunks and BORED APE YACHT CLUB as an example. If someone creates a cartoon using those images, those are now considered drawings and can have copyright protection. However, in that instance, the images are not being used to associate with a product or service. Thus, they are not considered trademarks. To illustrate this point in the real world, let's talk about the very well-known cartoon character: Mickey Mouse. Mickey was protected through copyright because it was a drawing. However, Mickey is also a trademark since there are several products and services that use Mickey as a source identified by Disney in the market. Thus, one drawing could function as a trademark and copyright at the same time. However, copyrights have a limited duration in time, while trademarks can be renewed every ten years if the mark is continued to be used in commerce.

Brands have experienced some challenges regarding trademark use for NFTs, which is why they are now running to register new trademarks for their digital products. Thus, the first task before launching an NFT project is to make sure that your brand is protected as a trademark in connection with selling digital products.

Recent Case Law Involving Trademarks and NFTs:

Hermès v. Rothschild[5]

In Hermès International et al. v. Mason Rothschild, which is one of the first trademark cases involving NFTs, the U.S. District Court for the Southern District of New York addressed trademark rights in connection with NFTs and digital assets. Hermès International, the owner of the famous BIRKIN trademark for luxury handbags, sued Mason Rothschild for trademark infringement after he created and sold NFTs of digital images of furry handbags, which he called "MetaBirkins." Rothschild sold the MetaBirkin NFTs during Miami Art Basel in 2021 for prices comparable to that of the Hermès BIRKIN handbags (i.e., tens of thousands of dollars).

In the dispute, the court considered whether Rothschild's use of the Hermés' trademark in his NFT could be considered noncommercial and, thus, an expression of art because the NFT is just a certificate. This was the question before the court because if Rothschild's use of the "MetaBirkins" bag is considered commercial use, then the rules regarding trademarks and, specifically, the likelihood of confusion would apply, and a potential trademark violation could be considered. In their decision, the court did not think Rothschild's NFTs in connection with the "MetaBirkin" digital images were "commercial." Instead, the court explained that

---

[5]https://www.lexology.com/library/detail.aspx?g=07c159e2-7053-45fa-a4c0-2dd72078ca4e&utm_source=Lexology+Daily+Newsfeed&utm_medium=HTML+email+-+Body+-+General+section&utm_campaign=Lexology+subscriber+daily+feed&utm_content=Lexology+Daily+Newsfeed+2022-05-26&utm_term=

NFTs are merely an authentication tool, meaning a code pointing to the location of digital images and authenticating the images, like a certificate. This case is very important because it will decide the future of NFTs and trademarks. This point is notable for brand owners seeking to enforce trademark rights against *virtual assets* that are usable in the metaverse bearing confusingly similar marks.

Nike v. StockX[6]

As intellectual property disputes over NFTs began to hit U.S. courts, including that involving Hermès discussed above, Nike, one of the world's most popular shoe brands, sued online reseller StockX in the United States District Court for the Southern District of New York for trademark infringement and dilution after StockX began selling NFT images of Nike sneakers without Nike's permission. Nike alleges that StockX's use is likely to cause consumer confusion and interfere with their own NFT plan. Whereas StockX argues that its use of NFTs containing images of Nike sneakers was "no different than major e-commerce retailers and marketplaces who use images and descriptions of products to sell physical sneakers and other goods, which consumers see (and are not confused by) every single day."

This court's future decision may shed light on how courts should treat the resale of physical products through NFTs and the likelihood of consumer confusion. If the court

---

[6]https://www.reuters.com/legal/litigation/stockx-strikes-back-nike-nft-lawsuit-2022-03-31/; https://www.lexology.com/library/detail.aspx?g=41a4315b-93b0-40b8-a45f-4ba46904ff0c;
https://www.lexology.com/library/detail.aspx?g=79e94411-d616-4e43-b7d7-0527f1a1f86b

considers StockX's use as virtual products or digital sneakers, there very well could be infringement. However, if the court determines that the NFTs are merely, as StockX argues, "claim tickets" to access physical shoes and provide proof of ownership and authenticity, the future of online resellers in the NFT world may be revolutionized. This dispute raises poignant questions concerning IP rights and potential defenses against infringement claims for use in NFTs. For instance, will this court hold StockX's NFTs as digital goods or digital receipts? If not, should StockX's resell use of Nike's trademark constitute fair use as it does in the physical world? Furthermore, do third-party resellers, like StockX, have different rights to the physical product as compared to a digital one without ancillary benefits? The list of questions goes on. While it remains to be seen, this decision has the potential to answer many pressing trademark questions in the world of NFTs.

Patents

Patents protect novel, nonobvious ideas that create a thing or process that is useful. For example, blockchain technology, which is the platform behind cryptocurrency and NFTs, is a process that could be the subject matter of a patent. There are three types of patents: utility, design, and plan. In order for you to have a patent, you need to file the patent application with the USPTO office. You can file a patent application with the USPTO on your behalf at www.uspto.gov or seek the help of a registered patent agent or attorney.

Patent protection grants its owner the exclusive right to exclude others from making, using, offering for sale, or selling his/her invention for a limited period of time (20 years). In the

NFT world, minting an NFT associated with an invention protected by a patent may lead to patent infringement. While there is no case law on point yet regarding this matter, we can use an example to better understand how this would play out in real life. For example, if a new company protects the design and underlying technical features associated with their products by patent, and a third decides to mint an NFT that ships that company's physical product to the NFT purchasers, that third person may be liable for patent infringement.

Trade Secrets

Trade Secrets are commercially valuable ideas that are unique to your business or that only you or a limited group of persons know. Unlike the other types of intellectual property, there is no centralized office that regulates or registers trade secrets. Trade secrets are only protected by the law if they are kept secret. In order to keep trade secrets protected, most owners use NDAs (non-disclosure agreements) and other reasonable steps to keep the information confidential.

Trade secrets law protects confidential information from unauthorized disclosure, use, or acquisition. Liability extends not only to the person who unlawfully discloses, uses, or acquires the information but also to any other person who uses or acquires such information knowing that the information was obtained or disclosed to them without the trade secrets' owner's authorization. In the NFT world, NFT creators and subsequent purchasers may be liable for trade secret infringement if the NFT includes unauthorized confidential information.

III.   NFTS AND SMART CONTRACTS - ARE THEY REAL CONTRACTS?

We cannot talk about IP and NFTs without understanding "smart contracts" because they are at the core of the sale of an NFT and IP. Smart contracts are not actually real contracts written in traditional legal language and format. They are computer codes stored on the blockchain that convert traditional contracts, written in traditional legal language and format, into digital parallels. Smart contracts are logical and follow an "if this, then that" structure. That means they behave exactly as programmed and cannot be changed.

The term "smart contract" was coined by Nick Szabo, a cryptographer. In 1994, Szabo first introduced the concept and, in 1996, delved more into what smart contracts could do.[7] As Szabo explains in "Contracts Embedded in the World:

The basic idea of smart contracts is that many kinds of contractual clauses (such as liens, bonding, delineation of property rights, etc.) can be embedded in the hardware and software we deal with in such a way as to make a breach of contract expensive (if desired, sometimes prohibitively so) for the breacher. A canonical real-life example, which we might consider to be the primitive ancestor of smart contracts, is the humble vending machine. Within a limited amount of potential loss (the amount in the till should be less than the cost of breaching the mechanism), the machine takes in coins, and via a simple mechanism, which makes a beginner's level problem in design with finite automata, dispense change and

---

[7] https://www.fon.hum.uva.nl/rob/Courses/InformationInSpeech/CDROM/Literature/LOTwinterschool2006/szabo.best.vwh.net/smart.contracts.html

https://www.fon.hum.uva.nl/rob/Courses/InformationInSpeech/CDROM/Literature/LOTwinterschool2006/szabo.best.vwh.net/smart_contracts_2.html *product fairly. Smart contracts go beyond the vending machine in proposing to embed contracts in all sorts of property that is valuable and controlled by digital means. Smart contracts reference that property in a dynamic, proactively enforced form and provide much better observation and verification where proactive measures must fall short. And where the vending machine, like electronic mail, implements an asynchronous protocol between the vending company and the customer, some smart contracts entail multiple synchronous steps between two or more parties.*[8]

As mentioned, smart contracts are immutable and, thus, can create some problems. In short, unlike real contacts, smart contracts are decentralized, meaning no one controls them or their terms. For example, in a contract sale between A and B, it is written that when B shall pay A. If B does not pay, then A and B file a lawsuit against B in court. In a smart contract, the same thing happens. However, the payment is automatic (i.e., if B pays, then the smart contract will automatically, and without intermediaries, transfer the property and complete the sale, but if it does not pay A, no contract is formed).

On the one hand, smart contracts have many useful applications because they enforce payment without the need for court action. For example, they can be used for payments of royalties in the case of the transfer of an IP, and the payment will be automatic, and if there is no payment, there is no IP transfer. On the other hand, they also pose risks, as they

---

[8]https://www.fon.hum.uva.nl/rob/Courses/InformationInSpeech/CDROM/Lite rature/LOTwinterschool2006/szabo.best.vwh.net/smart.contracts.html

https://www.fon.hum.uva.nl/rob/Courses/InformationInSpeech/CDROM/Liter ature/LOTwinterschool2006/szabo.best.vwh.net/smart_contracts_2.html are susceptible to code errors, bugs, protocol changes, platform problems, and upgrades, as well as are unresponsive to real-world issues (i.e., when something unexpected happens, the contract is immutable, and this can be a huge problem when something goes wrong).

It is important to note that while smart contracts are automated, lawyers still need to draft the initial, real contract that will be translated into code on the blockchain into a smart contract. From there, a key challenge with smart contracts is finding a trusted technical expert to either capture the parties' agreement in legal terms and then work with a coder to code or confirm that the code written by a third party is accurate. An interaction between the coder and the lawyer is necessary to make sure a good smart contract is drafted. The parties may also want written representations from the programmer that the code performs as contemplated. At the present time, there is no simple method to amend smart contracts. Unlike real-text contracts, where parties can quickly draft an amendment that addresses a specific change or course of conduct, smart contracts are immutable and far more complicated than simply modifying standard software code that does not reside on a blockchain.[9]

CryptoPunks and the Smart Contract "error"

We saw firsthand the practical importance of drafting a good (errorless) smart contract after Larva Labs, the owner of CryptoPunks NFTs, mistakenly offered the original collection of 10,000 CryptoPunks NFTs for free in 2017. The costly

---

[9]https://corpgov.law.harvard.edu/2018/05/26/an-introduction-to-smart-contracts-and-their-potential-and-inherent-limitations/

mistake was due to an error in the code of the smart contract that caused the *buyer* of a CryptoPunk NFT to receive back the proceeds of CryptoPunk resales, which in turn left the seller with nothing. As explained above, due to the nature of blockchain, Larva Labs could not simply fix or replace the error by updating the smart contract or erasing/replacing the problematic code. Instead, Larva Labs had to create a whole new collection governed by a completely new smart contract (i.e., one without the defect from the first). While the smart contracts governing the CryptoPunks NFTs are an excellent example of the complexity of smart contracts, they also illustrate how important it is to review the smart contract to ensure that it is automatically processing the terms and conditions you want. Unfortunately, long after finding the error in the code of the smart contract that caused the NFTs to be free, Larva Labs also learned that they initially offered the collection without any written content license or governing legal terms. Thus, in 2019, Larva Labs had to adopt an NFTs license to specify the limitations on its use, including, but not limited to, the right to display it on a marketplace for purchase, but not the right to create derivative works. From there, they also added a Terms and Conditions page to the CryptoPunks website in 2021.[10]

Considering that, when we are talking about IP and Smart Contracts, it is the smart contract's job to define whether IP transfers are connected to the sale of an NFT or not and how. In the IP world, there are two kinds of IP transfers that can be made. One is called an assignment, in which the IP

---

[10]https://www.lexology.com/library/detail.aspx?g=bdf380f9-04da-4eb3-b253-6a419cf955bd

holder transfers all of the IP rights and does not retain any rights at all. The other is called a license. Under a license, the IP holder still retains their IP rights but grants the buyer the right to use the IP. A license can be granted to a certain territory for a period of time and/or for a specific use or purpose, as well as other limitations to the use of the IP. In addition, it is important to note that an IP transfer needs to be in writing. If no writing exists, no IP transfer is made.

IV. WHAT SHOULD THE AVERAGE PERSON KNOW ABOUT IP BEFORE LAUNCHING AN NFT PROJECT?

People are making million-dollar NFT purchases without knowing what they are really buying and/or selling. This is due to, in part, the mass marketing and social media buzz surrounding NFTs and the fact that we just lived through an unprecedented pandemic that changed the way people consume. During the pandemic, the market had to find a way for people to continue to consume, and a virtual marketplace was the answer. NFTs were created to fulfill a consumer's need in the market. That said, everyone creating, buying, and selling NFTs in the blockchain should be careful and know the following:

For the creators: It is important to know **if your work has IP protection and if you really own the IP** behind the digital or physical asset you are creating into an NFT. For example, if you are selling a digital image, make sure you created that image independently and are not using anyone else's copyright material or trademark for commercial purposes.

Here is another scenario that the creator needs to be aware of when creating a digital image: when you use a computer program to create your digital asset, the program is owned by **a software company that allows you to create the artwork** and, thus, you may not own the copyright of the work you created using that software if the terms and conditions of that software say so. The creator should be sure that he/she is the owner of the digital product created through the software and that he/she owns the rights and not the software company. It is also important to remember that the work must be created by a human in order to be protected by copyright. Thus, you cannot copyright work made entirely by machines and virtual intelligence. Another issue not mentioned yet is the concept of "work for hire". If you are an employee and you created a digital image in the scope of your work for an employer, then you are the creator of the work but not the owner. Your employee is considered the owner, and you cannot sell the work you created through an NFT.

Additionally, the creator should determine if the digital asset he/she created is an original idea protected through copyright law. If so, it would be advisable **to register the work with the Copyright office** in order to protect it. If the idea is not original, he/she can utilize an NFT to show that the asset is original and authentic but does not have any real value because it is not protected by copyright.

Furthermore, NFT creators should make sure that **he/she protects the trademark** of the name of the characters and/or collections sold through an NFT. For example, let's imagine that CryptoPunks was already registered as a trademark by another party when the NFT project was created and sold. In that hypothetical situation, they would have to change their name because they cannot use another's trademark. Additionally, creators should make sure that they are not using third-party trademarks without the trademark owner's authorization when creating a digital image sold through an NFT for commercial purposes. If you use someone else's trademark, you could be sued by the trademark owner for infringement. It is always a good idea for creators to seek the help of a lawyer to make sure he/she understands what he/she is selling or wants to sell. Understanding what you are selling and if you can use someone else's trademark without authorization is essential to make sure you have a good smart contract to protect your rights.

Finally, when using smart contracts, creators should consult with a lawyer before putting the agreement into coding. The smart contract guarantees the enforceability of the contract but cannot foresee or advise you on exactly what problems you may have in the future with the other parties. Thus, a lawyer can help you make sure that these foreseeable issues are included in the code.

For sellers: Know exactly what you're selling. This includes making sure that a digital asset is not already protected by someone else's IP, especially in cases involving digital art or any other work protected by intellectual property. If you are not also the creator, you must do your due diligence to make sure that no other intellectual property was violated when the digital asset was created. Finally, make sure you read the smart contract and its terms to know exactly what you are selling.

For buyers: Know exactly what you are buying. You might be paying a lot of money for something that has no IP protection or no protection at all. Therefore, read **all of the**

contract terms of the purchase displayed online. If you are paying millions of dollars for digital art, you will want to know whether you were granted just a license to display the digital art without **commercial purpose or a license** or if the license includes a right to use the digital asset for commercial purposes. Also, you should know that if you are buying the IP through an **assignment,** then you own all the rights regarding digital art. However, remember that, similar to the fact that buying a physical painting or photograph from a well-known artist for a million dollars **does not mean** that you can reproduce that painting and sell it to third parties, you cannot reproduce or sell a digital asset without the owner's authorization. In most cases, you are just buying the right to display the digital art on your computer and **nothing else**.

<u>For all:</u> I remember back in 1999, during the Internet boom when people started registering other peoples' trademarks as domain names. McDonald's was one of the first cases where someone registered the trademark as a domain name and tried to sell it to McDonald's. At the time, I wrote a paper saying that the current trademark laws should apply to the unlawful use of other parties' domain names. Then, after that, during the Web2 boom, people started using other peoples' images without authorization and started placing those images on their websites and social media accounts to promote their products. From there, many people started to receive cease and desist letters to stop the use of those images because those images have copyright protection. The same is happening right now with Web3 as new IP creations are appearing, such as digital images and digital artwork. However, that does not mean that IP laws are obsolete. Rather, it means that one immersed in this new world should

have a basic understanding of the IP laws to make sure that one does not get in trouble for infringing such laws. In Web3, we will just have to adapt to the existing IP laws as new concepts continue to arise from the use of this new technology.

In sum, consult a lawyer to learn if you have an original idea protected by IP laws before launching your NFT project. Without IP protection, you will likely spend a lot of time and money trying to prove that you own the rights to the digital asset if someone steals the idea from you. Additionally, make sure a lawyer helps you draft the contract that will be encoded (the smart contract) to contain terms and conditions that you wish to be applicable. Using general "smart contracts" templates will likely help you guarantee that payment will be made, but they don't solve future real-world problems that could happen in the course of the agreement that computers cannot. Remember that smart contracts cannot think, and only the human mind can.

Other Books By The Author

The Power of Real-Time Social Media Marketing:
https://www.amazon.com/Power-Real-Time-Social-Media-Marketing-ebook/dp/B004G090HY

Description
The Power of Real-Time Social Media Marketing: How to Attract and Retain Customers and Grow the Bottom Line in the Globally Connected World

About The Author
Author Name: Beverly Macy

Imagine That... From PCs to NFTs is authored by Beverly Macy, a leading expert in the field of technology and its impact on business and society. Beverly has a unique perspective on the history of technology and its evolution. She has a deep understanding of the key innovations and disruptions that have shaped the tech industry and the ways in which technology is changing our world.

She currently teaches Media, Sports & Entertainment at UCLA Anderson School of Management and Brand Management at UCLAx. She launched one of the very first NFT courses on any college campus with her NFTs and Web3 in Business course in August 2022. The course attracted over 400 people to log in.

With her wealth of knowledge and experience as an educator and industry expert, Beverly is the perfect guide to take you on a journey through the history and future of technology and NFTs. *Imagine That... From PCs to NFTs* offers readers a unique, expert perspective on the technological advancements that have shaped our world and the potential of NFTs to change the way we think about ownership and value.

Acknowledgments

I would especially like to acknowledge and thank those who inspired me to start on this journey back in early 2021. Your encouragement, feedback, and expertise were invaluable in bringing this book to life.

I would also like to extend my sincerest gratitude to the visionary contributors to this work. Each and every Use Case author is representative of what it takes to truly make an impact with new thinking in business. I spent countless hours scouring the NFT and Web3 landscape for the 'best of the best' and I believe they each represent that here.

This journey would not have been possible without the support and guidance of my family, extended family, friends, and colleagues. You mean more to me than you know.

A very special thank you to Michela Gilli for believing in me and in this project from the very beginning. And a special tribute to our beloved Katia Bassi, who was a shining example of what it means to be a source of brilliance and inspiration to all who knew her and worked with her. It was an honor to be in her presence and she is greatly missed.

[1] https://www.firstversions.com/2015/03/ibm-personal-computer.html

[2] https://en.wikipedia.org/wiki/Wang_Laboratories

[3] https://www.youtube.com/watch?v=BvcdhrZl_l4

[4] https://cdn.arstechnica.net/wp-content/uploads/sites/3/2017/07/ibm-pc-5150-print-ad.jpg

[5] https://www.bairesdev.com/blog/the-creator-economy-in-2022/

[6] https://earthsky.org/earth/how-do-flocking-birds-move-in-unison/#:~:text=His%20work%20showed%20that%20bird,the%20flock%20in%20a%20wave.%E2%80%9D

[7] https://news.artnet.com/market/christies-nft-beeple-69-million-1951036

[8] https://theharrispoll.com/briefs/nfts-collectors-investors/

[9] https://vogue.sg/every-body-nft-vogue-singapore-metaartclub/

[10] https://news.adidas.com/originals/into-the-metaverse--how-we-got-here-and-where-we-are-headed/s/6ccb61cb-2135-453e-8626-ac3d56faab30

[11] https://www.designboom.com/tag/nft-non-fungible-token/

[12] https://www.digitalmusicnews.com/2021/05/11/live-nation-nfts/

[13] https://nft.tiffany.com/

[14] https://www.ledgerinsights.com/tag/bored-ape-yacht-club/

[15] https://thedefiant.io/nyc-building-opensea

[16] https://www.theverge.com/2021/5/11/22430254/cryptopunks-christies-sale-larva-labs

[17] https://www.amazon.com/Power-Real-Time-Social-Media-Marketing-ebook/dp/B004G090HY

[18] https://www.tbwachiatday.com/

[19] https://www.youtube.com/watch?v=VtvjbmoDx-I

[20] https://www.imdb.com/name/nm0000631/

[21] https://www.tbwachiatday.com/

[22] https://en.wikipedia.org/wiki/Xerox_Star

[23] https://spectrum.ieee.org/xerox-parc

[24] https://www.investopedia.com/ask/answers/08/dotcom-pets-dot-com.asp#:~:text=The%20company%20raised%20%2482.5%20million,such%20as%20dog%20food%20bags.

[25] https://en.wikipedia.org/wiki/Tulip_mania

[26] https://en.wikipedia.org/wiki/Beanie_Babies

[27] https://www.salesforce.com/news/press-releases/2019/11/19/lamborghini-accelerates-trust-and-authenticity-with-salesforce-2/

[28] https://trustees.tufts.edu/info/bios/ho/

[29] https://www.youtube.com/watch?v=X_cRD784d4M

[30] https://www.uclaextension.edu/business-management/leadership-management/course/nfts-and-web3-business-mgmt-721

[31] https://www.grandviewresearch.com/industry-analysis/loyalty-management-market-report

[32] https://boredapeyachtclub.com/#/terms

[33] https://www.forbes.com/sites/cathyhackl/2021/09/25/caa-signs-jenkins-the-valet-is-this-a-sign-that-hollywood-is-embracing-nfts/?sh=89facce3b02d

[34] https://time.com/collection/timepieces-nft/

[35] https://www.netflix.com/title/81441273

[36] https://opensea.io/collection/boredapeyachtclub

[37] https://www.jenkinsthevalet.com/

[38] https://www.spottiewifi.io/

[39] https://opensea.io/collection/tribally

[40] https://www.vaneck.com/us/en/nftcommunity/events/

[41] https://ccaf.io/cbeci/index

[42] https://www.theblockcrypto.com/linked/130874/solana-nft-total-sales-volume-crosses-1-billion

[43] https://www.forbes.com/advisor/investing/cryptocurrency/what-is-ethereum-ether/

[44] https://www.forbes.com/advisor/investing/cryptocurrency/bitcoins-energy-usage-explained/

[45] https://www.pledge.to/crypto-donations

[46] http://www.threesquaresinc.com/

[47] https://www.globenewswire.com/en/news-release/2022/04/21/2426772/0/en/Earth-Day-Pledge-Becomes-the-First-Platform-to-Take-a-Stand-for-Environmentally-Conscious-Crypto-Donations.html#:~:text=While%20the%20final%20emissions%20will,carbon%20dioxide%20(CO2)%20emissions.

[48] https://unfccc.int/climate-action/climate-neutral-now

[49] https://blog.cryptoflies.com/st-jude-hospital-is-set-to-enter-the-metaverse-and-embrace-nfts/

[50] https://clutchwallet.xyz/

[51] https://venturebeat.com/games/parsons-school-of-design-and-roblox-partner-up-for-digital-fashion/

[52] https://www.imdb.com/title/tt1677720/

[53] https://www2.deloitte.com/us/en/pages/technology/articles/what-does-the-metaverse-mean.html

[54] http://www.opensea.com

33695669R00111